The Treasures
of the Mass

The Treasures of the Mass

A devotional explanation of the prayers, ceremonies and mysteries of the Holy Sacrifice, and the benefits to be derived through devout participation.

Laudamus press

Copyright © 2015 by Laudamus Press/Hillside Education

Originally published in 1936
by Benedictine Convent of Perpetual Adoration

Nihil Obstat

☩ Stephanus Schappler, O.S.B.
Abbas Coadjutor Im. Conceptionis

Imprimatur

☩ Carolus Hubertus Le Blond
Episcopus Sancti Josephi

All rights reserved. No part of this publication may be reproduced in whole or in part, stored in a retrieval system or transmitted in any form or by any means, electronic, mechanical, photocopying, recording, or otherwise, without prior written permission of the publisher.

Cover image: *The Last Supper* by Juan de Juanes, circa 1560

Cover design by Mary Jo Loboda

ISBN: 978-0-9906720-4-3

Laudamus Press
P.O. Box 251
Hamlin, PA 18427
www.laudamus-te.com

Translation of Latin texts: To Thee be praise, to Thee be glory, to Thee be thanksgiving. May our Sacrifice ascend to Thee, O Lord, and may Thy mercy descend upon us.

This picture and its inscriptions tell us that Holy Mass is our most perfect means of rendering praise and thanks to the Triune God and of imploring His gifts and graces. Let us daily employ this precious means.

Foreword

OVER a quarter of a century ago, Pope Pius X of blessed memory sounded the watchword of the Liturgical Movement in the pithy phrase "Pray the Mass." Our generation has seen a marvelous growth of that movement, and its most noteworthy fruit has been a great reawakening among the faithful of a true and intelligent appreciation of the central act of Catholic worship, the holy Sacrifice of the Mass.

The Treasures of the Mass is a splendid contribution to the work of the Liturgical Revival, because it is a simple yet sound and thorough explanation of the meaning of the Mass and its ceremonial. Its style and manner of presentation are well adapted to the intellectual capacity of the ordinary lay Catholic, and yet it so abounds in inspiring information that it will be read with interest and profit even by priests.

May God bless this little work and multiply its fruit for the sanctification of souls.

✠ *Charles Hubert Le Blond*
Bishop of St. Joseph

May 19, 1936

Contents

Foreword... vii
Introduction 1

I. Mass of the Catechumens

The Ambassador of Christ 15
    Dignity and Power of the Priest 16
At the Foot of the Altar 18
    A Plea for Pardon 21
    Comfiteor 21
At the Altar 23
    Introit 24
    Kyrie 25
Joy in God 28
    Gloria 28
    Dominus Vobiscum 30
    Collect 31
Heralds Prepare the Way 33
    Epistle 34
    Gradual 36
    Tract and Sequence 37
    Gospel 39
The Torch of Faith 43
    Nicene Creed 43
    The Substance of Our Belief 45
    The Fruit of the Gospel 46

II. Mass of the Faithful

Gifts to the Most High 49
    Offertory 49
    The Spotless Host 51
    Mingling of Water and Wine 52
    The Chalice of Salvation 54
    Washing of the Hands 55
    Oblation to the Holy Trinity 57
    Orate, Fratres 59
    Holy Mass—My Sacrifice 60
    Secret 62
    Preface 63

Amid Angel Throngs 66
    Sanctus and Benedictus 66
Prayers before the "Great Wonder" 68
    The Canon 68
    Prayer of Oblation for the Church *(Te igitur)* 69
    Where Remembrance Is Precious *(Commemoration of the Living)* 72
    "Fellow-citizens with the Saints" *(Communicantes)* 74
    A Fourfold Petition *(Hanc Igitur)* 77
    Bloody and Unbloody Sacrifice Identified by the Cross *(Quam Oblationem)*. . . 78
The Heart of the Mass 80
    Consecration and Elevation 80
    "My Lord and My God!" 82
    Jesus, Our Mediator 85
    "Hail, Precious Blood!" 87
    Souls Sprinkled with the Precious Blood 90
    Mystical Death of Christ 91
    O Wonder of Wonders! 92
    "Do This in Commemoration of Me!" 94
Hail, Victim Slain 95
    Offering of the "Pure, Holy, and Immaculate Victim"
        (First Prayer after the Consecration) 95
    The Most Acceptable Oblation *(Second Prayer after the Consecration)* 98
    When the Angels Intercede *(Third Prayer after the Consecration)* 100
    Unfailing Succor of the Departed *(Memento for the Dead)* 104
    Commemoration of the Church Militant *(Nobis Quoque Peccatoribus)* 107
    "Through Him, and with Him and in Him" *(Minor Elevation)* 109
The Breaking of Bread 112
    Pater Noster 113
    A Solemn Compact 115
    Supplication for Peace *(Libera)* 117
    The Breaking of the Sacred Host 121
    A Threefold Peace 123
    Mingling of the Species 124
The Divine Lamb of Sacrifice 125
    Agnus Dei 125
    The Three Prayers after the Agnus Dei 128
The Eucharistic Banquet 132
    The Priest's Communion 132
    Communion of the Faithful 135
    Mutual Longing Satisfied 138
    The Ablution Prayers 141
    Communion Antiphon 144
    Postcommunion 145
Conclusion of the Mass 146
    "Ite, Missa Est" 147
    "Deo Gratias" 148
    Prayer to the Holy Trinity 150
    The Last Blessing 151

 The Last Gospel..153
 Concluding Prayers..156
ARTICLES USED FOR HOLY MASS AND THEIR SPIRITUAL SIGNIFICANCE....158
 The Altar and Its Furnishings...160
 The Sacred Vessels...163
 Linens and Coverings for the Sacred Vessels...........................167
 The Sacred Vestments..169
 The Liturgical Colors 180
ASSISTING AT HOLY MASS..182
 Benefits Derived from Assisting at Mass...............................185
 Some Helpful Reminders...197
ACTS OF OBLATION 205
 Morning Offering 205
 Offering before Holy Mass..206

Introduction

Between Heaven and Earth

He Almighty God is, in Himself, eternal happiness. Therefore nothing can be wanting to Him. Were something lacking to Him, He would no longer be God, in whom all perfection dwells. And still, there was a time when God called the wonderful universe into existence. Millions and millions of blessed spirits now surround Him in heaven. A host of suns and myriads of stars form, as it were, a *via triumphalis* — a triumphal way, on which He treads. On our earth, the three kingdoms of nature: the animal, plant and mineral kingdoms, of which He made man the king, proclaim His wisdom and power, His beauty and goodness.

Considering this, we involuntarily ask ourselves: *For what reason did God, to whom nothing is wanting, create all this beauty, and call these many creatures into existence?* Reason and faith answer: God did it *out of purest love and goodness*, out of Divine generosity. He did not wish to enjoy His bliss and happiness alone; He desired that other beings should share His glory and His riches. For this reason He called creation into existence.

Duty of Adoration

GOD is the Creator. Man, the creature, is the work of His hands, His possession. It is the duty of man to *consider the Creator as his supreme Lord and Master, to prostrate in reverence and admiration before Him; to adore and praise Him.*

To adore the Divinity, to pay homage to God—what an honor for a poor creature! To acknowledge in God all good, all truth, all that is worthy of affection; to submit one's understanding and will to God's greatness; to offer Him one's soul and body; yea, even to wish to consume oneself in order to procure Him honor and glory — can there be a nobler aim in life?

God not only called the universe into being but He also *preserves* it *continually.* This constant preservation is no less a miracle than the creation itself. Were the Creator to withdraw His hand for but one instant from His work of creation, the great universe would return to nothingness; so too would every individual creature.

Hence, God thinks of us, His creatures, at every moment; He provides for us from day to day and preserves us with infinite love.

He holds in store for us everything good, everything lovely and beautiful, for it is His glory to share His happiness; He wishes us to participate in it. He has made our earthly life like unto that of paradise; His whole creation He places at our feet. If we find thorns and thistles, it is not God's fault. Sin, willful sin, has spoiled everything. The malice of original sin and of the many personal sins of mankind is the sole cause of our sufferings and trials here below.

However, God in His infinite mercy and goodness has destined that these very sufferings and trials should become a source of merit and future happiness for us through His beloved Son. Jesus has ennobled and sanctified suffering through His Cross. Is it not just, then, that we should prove ourselves grateful for His Divine

Providence, for the preservation of our life, for the many benefits He bestows upon us?

God's Right to Our Gratitude

GOD *has a strict claim to the gratitude of His creatures.* Gratitude should incessantly ascend to Him from the hearts of men, because God's providence is without limits, and God's love operates continually for us. Just as each moment of our life is a new benefit from God, so should it be a renewed thanksgiving toward our benevolent Creator. *Benefits demand gratitude.* Oh, that man would have the understanding and good will to think of his great Benefactor often during the day and often during the night—his life would become an uninterrupted hymn of thanks. But alas! how different is the reality! What a misfortune for man!

Instead of adoring his Lord and Creator and thanking Him, man offends Him fearlessly and impudently to His face. He sins every day! The helpless creature offends an Almighty God! Sin is contempt of God, revolt against God, and exacts from the Creator the exercise of His right to demand an account from the sinner, to punish him, and refuse him pardon until he is sorry, does penance, and makes satisfaction.

God's Right to Satisfaction

GOD is infinitely good, but likewise infinitely just. *He will not yield His right of demanding satisfaction from the sinner.* God cannot allow a haughty creature to despise His commands and break His laws with impunity. His dignity and sanctity cannot tolerate this. Not to punish the sinner would mean to disregard sin, and, indirectly, to approve of it; it would mean to discourage the good. A father who does not punish the child that is indulging in vice and showing no signs of amendment — is such a father to be considered a good father? Sad to say, all too many people look at sin in a different light. But God must punish sin; hence sinful man—and we all are sinners—must render *satisfaction*, or live and die an enemy of God and be forever separated from Him.

Necessity of Prayer

GOD gives to man the life of the body, and, in Holy Baptism, the far more precious supernatural life of grace. If our natural life cannot continue even for one moment without Divine Providence, much less can the life of grace be retained without Divine assistance. Did not God's generosity always accompany man with His blessings, how would he ever attain to eternal blessedness? What is man without the grace of God? Grace, however, is a free gift of God; God even desires to lavish grace upon us. We need thousands of graces for obtaining life eternal, and we must *ask* for them; that is the Divine will; hence, *the necessity of prayer.*

God has created and redeemed us without our meriting these benefits; but He will not give us eternal happiness without our co-operation. We must merit heaven. He expects that we toil for Him. He expects our co-operation with His grace and our co-operation by good works. This co-operation is to be of our own free will, not forced. Were God to do all, and we nothing toward our eternal salvation, where would be our merit? Where our claim to reward? Or, if God were to force us, where would be our liberty in our actions? God leaves every man *free* to decide for good or evil, and, according to this choice we meet with good and wicked men in this world. If we choose the good and perform it, we acquire merits for heaven. However, of ourselves we can neither will nor accomplish any good; for this we need the assistance of God. "Without Me you can do nothing," said Our Lord (John 15: 5). We must ask for this assistance, for this grace of graces. In other words, *we must pray.*

Four Claims and Four Duties

WHAT has been said in the foregoing paragraphs regarding the mutual relations of God and man, the Creator and the creature, may be briefly summed up as follows:—

1. God is the supreme good, the Creator of all things, the most holy One. Therefore man owes God, in the first place, *adoration.*
2. God is the origin and motive of good; He is the Author of all man is and has. Hence, man must show *gratitude* toward God, his greatest Benefactor.
3. God is offended by sin. Therefore the sinner must ask His pardon and render *satisfaction for sin.*
4. God has decreed to give His special graces only to those who ask Him for them. Therefore, man must *pray* to obtain these graces and to live in grace.

Thus we see that from the four claims of God upon His creatures, arise four duties of the creature toward his Creator. But we, poor children of Eve, how can we fulfill these duties? Are we at all capable of fulfilling them so as to win the approval of God? To this there can be but one answer: *No.* We have become so helpless through sin that even with the best of will and the greatest exertion it would be impossible, of our own strength, to regain the friendship of God. Our adoration will never correspond to the infinite majesty of God, nor our gratitude to the benefits we have received; our satisfaction could never repair the insult and contempt we have offered to the Supreme Being; and our prayer, alas! our poor, distracted prayer, could of itself never reach the throne of God, could never merit to be heard. There is a deep abyss between the almighty, thrice-holy, eternal God and His poor sinful creatures.

Since we cannot, of ourselves, comply with our four principal duties to God, what remains to be done?

The Unspotted Lamb

BEHOLD! In the midst of this desert of sinfulness and helplessness there arises before our eyes *an altar*. A priest ascends the steps; a supernatural, indelible mark is impressed upon his soul. He places upon the altar a chalice and a host. From his lips proceed a few omnipotent words which he pronounces over this chalice and this host—and, O wonder! the Body and Blood of the Son of God are present upon the altar. Earth awakens, its exiled children arise; they draw nearer and nearer; they gather about the altar, and from millions and millions of hearts ascend humble and grateful prayers. Songs of praise resound; fervent petitions are heard; and from on high, from heaven's heights, resound melodies that betoken love and forgiveness, blessings and joy. Heavenly spirits proclaim glory to God and peace to men.

What has happened? Why this jubilation, this hope? Mankind has offered upon the altar the pure, unspotted Lamb to the Eternal Father. By this Sacrifice mankind worthily acknowledges God's sovereign rights, thanks Him for His gifts, renders atonement for its misdeeds and petitions His help. The Eternal Father accepts the sacrifice of His Son, the homage of mankind: *It is Holy Mass*—the rescuing oasis where, as on another Calvary, God and man meet and offer friendship's hand.

The Sacrifice of Calvary Perpetuated

THE Sacrifice of the Cross was the greatest act which the Divine and human love of Jesus Christ accomplished for us. Through the death of Christ on the Cross we were redeemed. Through His immolation on the Cross, the Lamb of God took away the sins of the world and reconciled mankind with the Heavenly Father. No further sacrifice of redemption was necessary. However, the Sacrifice of our Savior on the Cross did not do away with the personal duty of His creatures to pay unto their God and Creator the highest form of outward worship possible to man—*sacrifice*. Otherwise man's worship would have been shorn of its most important feature, its highest and principal function. Therefore the unfathomable love and wisdom of the Savior provided a means of daily *renewing* the Sacrifice of the Cross in the holy Sacrifice of the Mass. The Sacrifice of the Cross merited for us immeasurable treasures of grace; through Holy Mass these graces are applied to our souls.

Holy Mass is, according to the teaching of Holy Church, the *same* Sacrifice as that which our Savior offered on the Cross, differing only in the *manner of offering*. "The *same* Sacrifice!" Who can fully grasp the purport of these words? Yet they are true, nevertheless, for in Holy Mass we have the same *Priest* and the same *Victim* as in the Sacrifice of Calvary. On the Cross, Jesus Christ offered Himself by shedding His Blood and meriting for us; on our altars He sacrifices Himself through the ministry of the priest, *without shedding His Blood,* and *applies to us the fruits of His Passion and Death.* The Sacrifice of the Mass does not increase the merits of the Sacrifice of the Cross; it *applies* them to souls.

Since Holy Mass is a renewal of the Sacrifice of the Cross, it follows that Holy Mass is the most sublime means of honoring God and the richest fountain of grace and blessings for the Church and for the faithful. A spiritual writer says: "Just as the sun surpasses, all other planets in brightness and strength, and brings more benefit to the earth than all the stars combined, so the Sacrifice of the Mass surpasses all other works of devotion."

Holy Mass possesses an *infinite value*. The Heavenly Father looked with infinite complacency upon His Divine Son when He accomplished the Sacrifice of the Cross. With the same complacency His eye rests upon every altar whereon the holy Sacrifice of the Mass is offered. From each altar a stream of graces flows out over the whole Church of Christ. Ceaselessly we can draw from this stream of grace in Holy Mass for our life on earth and for our glory in eternity. How great is the loss that one suffers who passes through life without drawing from this ocean of graces, to which he may so easily have access, the blessings which he needs to make him truly happy! Jesus on our altars offers us His help and His consolations, His blessing and His peace, His goodness and His joy, His sufferings and His Death, with all their merit. He yearns to come to our assistance in our needs, and whose need is not great?

Means of Fulfilling Our Fourfold Duty

THROUGH the Holy Sacrifice we can perfectly fulfill our fourfold duty toward God. This spotless Sacrifice redounds to *God's greatest honor and glory*. It is likewise the most perfect sacrifice of *adoration and praise* that the Majesty of God can demand. We can offer this Sacrifice to *thank God* for all the graces which He has granted to ourselves, to those near to us, to the Church, to all mankind, as well as those which He has granted and will continue to grant to all the saints and angels for all eternity. We can also offer this Holy Sacrifice *to make atonement* for our own sins and for the sins of the whole world. This Sacrifice of priceless worth we may also offer *to implore blessing, grace and protection* for ourselves, for our dear ones, for the Church and for all mankind as also for the relief of the souls in purgatory.

Would to God that we appreciated aright the immense treasure which we possess in Holy Mass! How happy we should then be! How zealously we should embrace every opportunity to hear Mass, and how attentively we should assist at its celebration! Too many Catholics look upon attendance at Mass only as an obligation; they fulfill that obligation largely through a sense of duty and only when the law of the Church prescribes attendance. Alas! of what treasures do those Catholics deprive themselves who absent themselves from Holy Mass when they could so easily be present each morning at its celebration!

Ah, how shall we excuse ourselves before God on the day of judgment for having neglected to assist at Holy Mass on account of our often trivial occupations, or our love of ease? It is true, we are not *commanded* to hear Mass on weekdays and God will not condemn us for not doing so. But may He not accuse us of being slothful in His service, and of wasting the talent of grace which was confided to our keeping— that is, the graces which would have been communicated to us through daily Holy Mass? May these humble pages inspire many souls with a deeper understanding and a more ardent love of the Holy Sacrifice, and urge them to assist more *frequently*, more *fervently*, and more *fruitfully* at its celebration!

He gave to the weak His Body as food, and He gave to the sad the cup of His Blood.

Dedit fragílibus córporis férculum, Dedit et trístibus sánguinis póculum. (Thomas Aquinas)

Courtesy of Campion Missal and Hymnal

The Structure of the Mass

THE first part of the Mass is a kind of introductory service, made up of chants, prayers and lessons (i.e. readings from Holy Scripture)—namely, the *Introit*, the *Kyrie*, the *Collect*, the *Epistle* or *Lesson*, and the *Gospel*. On certain days the *Gloria* and the *Nicene Creed* are added. This first part of the Mass is called the Mass of the Catechumens, while the remaining part is called the Mass of the Faithful. These names have their origin in the discipline of the early Church. In the first ages of Christianity, persons desiring to become Christians were obliged to undergo a course of instructions preparatory to baptism. They were called "catechumens," a Greek word meaning "one who is being instructed." Such persons, being not yet fully initiated in the teachings and practices of Christianity, were dismissed before the sacrificial part of the Mass commenced. Likewise, those who were undergoing a course of penance and had not yet been admitted to Communion were ordered to leave the church at this part of the Mass. That which followed was considered too holy for the presence of notorious sinners, and too mysterious to permit those to assist who were not yet fully instructed. Only those who were baptized—"the Faithful"—could take part in the actual Eucharistic Sacrifice. The Church, during the course of centuries, changed her discipline in this regard, and all are now permitted to remain during the entire sacred rite.

It may be interesting also to note the subdivisions of the parts of the Mass given in the St. Andrew's Missal. Be it understood, however, that the Mass is not a series of acts loosely joined together; the Mass is one continuous action, reproducing in a mysterious way the Life, Passion and Death of Jesus Christ. These subdivisions are intended only as an

aid in studying the Mass by an enumeration of the various parts which go to make up the whole. They are as follows:—
1. The *Preparation*—which includes the prayers at the foot of the altar, the *Introit*, *Kyrie* and *Gloria*.
2. The *Instruction*—which includes the *Collect*, the *Epistle*, *Gradual*, *Alleluia* (or *Tract*, and on certain feasts the *Sequence*), the *Gospel* (often followed by a sermon), and the *Credo*.
3. The *Oblation* — which includes the *Offertory* antiphon, the offering of bread, the pouring of water and wine into the chalice, the offering of the chalice, the washing of the hands, the prayer to the Blessed Trinity, the "Orate Fratres," and the *Secret*.
4. The *Consecration*—which includes the *Preface* and the *Canon* of the Mass, embracing the prayer "Te Igitur," the Memento of the Living, the *Communicantes* and the other two prayers before the Consecration, the *Consecration* and *Elevation*, the three prayers after the Consecration, the Commemoration of the Dead, the "Nobis quoque peccatoribus," and the Minor Elevation. (This part is, properly speaking, also a part of the oblation or sacrifice offering.)
5. The *Communion* — which includes the *Pater Noster*, the *Libera*, the *Agnus Dei*, the three prayers before the Communion, the "Domine non sum dignus," and the Communion of the Priest and the Faithful.
6. The *Thanksgiving* — which includes the *Communion* antiphon, the *Postcommunion* prayer, the "Ite missa est," and the *Last Gospel*.

Ordinary and Proper of the Mass

THE Mass consists of a fixed framework into which at certain points the variable prayers, lessons and chants are fitted. The former is called the *ordinary* or *common* of the Mass, and the latter, the *proper*.[1] The variable or proper parts of the Mass are the following: The *Introit, Collect, Epistle, Gradual, Alleluia* (or *Tract,* and on some feasts the *Sequence*), the *Gospel, Offertory, Secret, Communion and Postcommunion.* All the other parts remain the same in each Holy Mass except the *Preface,* which occupies an intermediate place between the changeable and unchangeable parts. Certain feasts and seasons have their own proper Preface, which changes after the introductory sentence. A common Preface is arranged for all days which do not have a proper Preface of their own. Similarly, a special clause is inserted in the prayer of the Canon called the *Communicantes,* on certain of the principal feasts.

Because the parts of the Mass vary, we speak of the Mass of such a day or of such a feast. In order to follow the changeable parts of the Mass, it is necessary to have a Missal, in which the proper parts of the Mass for each day and feast are given.

---

[1] *In our explanation of the Mass we have used the proper of the Mass of Corpus Christi, in honor of the Blessed Sacrament, which is one of the most beautiful combinations of psalms, prayers and hymns in the Catholic liturgy.*

I.
Mass of the Catechumens

The Ambassador of Christ

ALL the preparations for the Holy Sacrifice are completed; the altar is in readiness; a throng of devout souls, absorbed in God, is in expectation. A solemn stillness reigns in the house of God. The soft light of two blessed candles scarcely dispels the shadows of the morning twilight. Footsteps break the hallowed stillness. A priest comes forth in an attire set apart for the Divine service, and with serious mein. Slowly and reverently he approaches the altar, genuflects, ascends the steps, places the veiled chalice he carries in his hand upon the corporal, moves to the Epistle side and opens the missal. He then returns to the center of the altar. Inclines to the Crucifix, descends the steps, and begins the most sublime of rituals—Holy Mass.

Who is this priest? He may have come from a wealthy home, from the quiet of a farm, or from the noise of a workshop; his cradle may have stood in some cottage, or in a splendid mansion in the midst of a surging metropolis—all this signifies nothing and alters nothing in the eminent nature and sublimity of his mission. That which invests him with this singular dignity and greatness is not from men: God Himself has impressed upon his soul a mysterious, indelible mark which places him above all the mighty ones of earth. Heaven has given him a special mission and authority; hence, every door is open to him among Catholic people; to them he is the ambassador of Christ, a priest, who has the right to ascend the steps of the altar.

When God wishes to give us commands, promises, admonitions or graces, He makes use, not of an angel, but of a *priest*. Everything must pass through the hands of this extraordinary man. And woe to the one who despises his office and mission, who persecutes him, or grieves him! Woe! For such a man despises God Himself, persecutes God Himself, offends God Himself. Jesus declared this in a solemn manner. But happy the Christian who honors priests! Happy the family that receives him! Thus the priest is God's ambassador to man; but he is, at the same time, man's ambassador to God.

Dignity and Power of the Priest

AN ambassador of God! How often from the pulpit has he announced heavenly tidings to the faithful! How often spoken to them of their binding obligations, of imperishable hopes, of eternal rewards and everlasting punishments! Now he ascends the altar. In a little while he will speak mysterious words of astounding power, and the almighty, immortal God, obeying his call, will descend from heaven upon the altar. He will raise Him aloft in his hands before the kneeling worshipers, and give Him to souls who believe in Him, long for Him, seek Him, love Him, and wish to live through Him.

The priest, in union with Jesus Christ, offers man's *adoration, thanksgiving, expiation,* and *petition* to the heavenly Father, who receives this gift with complacency. In our name and for our salvation the priest offers to the Eternal Father His only-begotten Son Jesus; he offers to God the infinite merits of Jesus' life on earth, and especially His sacrificial death on Calvary. What angel of God can compare with the priest in greatness and dignity?

The priest negotiates with God on the most momentous questions of life—on the affairs of the soul. He raises his absolving hand, pronounces words of forgiveness, and the burden of sin is lifted from the repentant soul. He stands at the bedside of the dying, and equips the departing soul with the means to wage successfully its last combat. It is his word that seals and gives validity to the covenant of peace which is daily made between earth and heaven.

Kings and rulers of this earth frequently experience that the sceptre is snatched from their hand, the royal purple torn from their shoulders, and they themselves sent into exile. But the priest, the ambassador of Christ, remains a priest *forever.* God will never deprive him of his office. Of all ambassadors who speak and act in the name of a sovereign, the Catholic priest alone can, until his dying breath, treat with his Master with full authority in behalf of mankind, and with mankind in the name of God. Do we think of his exalted dignity when we meet a priest on the street, or see him at the altar in the act of celebrating Mass?

At the Foot of the Altar

BY HIS first act, the priest, the ambassador of God, convinces the people of the lawfulness of the office which he is now exercising. He genuflects, makes the Sign of the Cross and solemnly utters the words: —

In nomine Patris, et Filii et Spiritus Sancti. Amen.	In the Name of the Father, and of the Son, and of the Holy Ghost. Amen.

Is there, in the solemn services of the Catholic Church, another moment when these words, so simple, so frequently used, imply such majesty and sublimity as here at the foot of the altar, at the beginning of Holy Mass? Can the priest give us a more solemn explanation of his mission? To appear in the Name and with the authority of the eternal, almighty Creator—this, O Priest of God, is thy portion alone! Alone thy dignity and power, O Anointed of the Lord!

The priest joins his hands and continues:—

℣. *Introibo ad altare Dei.*	℣. I will go unto the altar of God.
℟. *Ad Deum qui laetiflcat juventutem meam.*	℟. Unto God who giveth joy to my youth.

Behold the young priest with the holy oils still fresh upon his consecrated hands. The moment for which he has been longing for years has arrived; he stands before the holy altar.

He signs himself with the sacred Cross, and the first exultant words that escape his lips are: "I will go unto the altar of God, unto God, who giveth joy to my youth!" —beautiful expression of a soul that has clung to God, who has led him to the mount of sacrifice; heavenly expression of love for God, for whom he has despised all worldly and sinful pleasures, to find his joy in Him.

Day after day these words surge up from the heart of the minister of God. Years pass. Maturity is reached with its experience, and perhaps, honors; old age steals on with its rich harvest and its peculiar trials; yet the same lips pronounce the same exultant words: "I will go unto the altar of God, unto God, who giveth joy to my youth." And when the Anointed of the Lord shall stand at the threshold of eternity, when the vision of the Immolated Lamb shall break upon his purified soul in all its dazzling beauty, will not his lips once more exclaim: "I will go unto the altar of God, unto God, who giveth joy to my youth!" But now his feet must still tread the weary paths of earth, and mindful of his own weakness, the priest presents his petitions in the words of the royal Psalmist (Ps. 42), which he prays alternately with the server, or, in the case of a dialogue Mass, with the congregation: —

℣. *Judica me, Deus, et discerne causam meam de gente non sancta; ab homine iniquo et doloso erue me.*	Judge me, O God, and distinguish my cause from the nation that is not holy; deliver me from the unjust and deceitful man.
℞. *Quia tu es, Deus, fortitude mea: quare me repulisti, et quare tristis incedo, dum affligit me inimicus?*	For Thou, O God, art my strength; why hast Thou cast me off? and why do I go sorrowful whilst the enemy afflicteth me?
℣. *Emitte lucem tuam et veritatem tuam; ipsa me deduxerunt et adduxerunt in montem sanctum tuum, et in tabernacula tua.*	Send forth Thy light and Thy truth: they have conducted me and brought me unto Thy holy hill, and into Thy tabernacles.

℟. Et introibo ad altare Dei: ad Deum qui laetificat juventutem meam.	And I will go unto the altar of God; unto God who giveth joy to my youth.
℣. Confitebor tibi in cithara, Deus, Deus meus: quare tristis es, anima mea, et quare conturbas me?	I will praise Thee upon the harp, O God, my God: why art thou sad, O my soul, and why dost thou disquiet me?
℟. Spera in Deo, quoniam adhuc confitebor illi: salutare vultus mei, et Deus meus.	Hope in God, for I will still give praise to Him: the salvation of my countenance, and my God.
℣. Gloria Patri, et Filio, et Spiritui Sancto.	Glory be to the Father, and to the Son, and to the Holy Ghost.
℟. Sicut erat in principle, et nunc, et semper: et in saecula saeculorum. Amen.	As it was in the beginning, is now, and ever shall be, world without end. Amen.

This is a touching supplication which the priest makes to Almighty God, to detach his sentiments from the spirit of the world and from his own corrupt nature; to keep him on the steep and narrow path and smooth away the difficulties on the way to the holy mount. Conscious of his own weakness, he trusts in God, his "strength"; he begs to be led by His "Light," Jesus Christ, the true Light which enlightens every man who comes into this world, and His "Truth," the Spirit of Truth, who proceeds from the Father and teaches us all truth, — confident that he will thus reach his eternal destination. The priest promises the Most High to make known to men the Divine precepts. He entrusts to God the sorrow and grief which overwhelm his soul, but likewise the hopes that fill his heart.

The Antiphon "Introibo" is then repeated.[2] Thereupon the celebrant makes the Sign of the Cross and protests that he places all his trust in the Name and in the help of God: —

---

[2] *In Masses for the dead and during Passiontide, the Psalm "Judica" is omitted, and the Antiphon "Introibe" is not repeated.*

At the Foot of the Altar

℣. Adjutorium nostrum in nomine Domini.
℟. Qui fecit coelum et terram.

℣. Our help is in the Name of the Lord.
℟. Who made heaven and earth.

A Plea for Pardon

*A*T the same moment, the realization of his own unworthiness overpowers the priest; he remembers his past sins, for, though vested with unearthly power, he is still merely a creature. In the consciousness of his guilt, he bends low before the altar and strikes his breast in all humility as he prays the act of contrition known as the

Confiteor

Confiteor Deo omnipotenti, beatae Mariae semper Virgini, beato Michaeli Archangelo, beato Joanni Baptistae, sanctis Apostolis Petro et Paulo, omnibus Sanctis, et vobis, fratres: quia peccavi nimis cogitatione, verbo et opere: mea culpa, mea culpa, mea maxima culpa. Ideo precor beatam Mariam semper Virginem, beatum Michaelem Archangelum, beatum Joannem Baptistam, sanctos Apostolos Petrum et Paulum, omnes sanctos, et vos, fratres, orare pro me ad Dominum Deum nostrum.

I confess to Almighty God, to blessed Mary ever Virgin, to blessed Michael the Archangel, to blessed John the Baptist, to the holy Apostles Peter and Paul, to all the saints, and to you brethren, that I have sinned exceedingly in thought, word and deed: through my fault, through my fault, through my most grievous fault. Therefore I beseech blessed Mary ever Virgin, blessed Michael the Archangel, blessed John the Baptist, the Holy Apostles Peter and Paul, all the saints, and you, brethren, to pray to the Lord our God for me.

The acolyte answers:—

Misereatur tui omnipotens Deus, et dimissis peccatis tuis, perducat te ad vitam aeternam.

May Almighty God have mercy upon thee, forgive thee thy sins, and bring thee to life everlasting.

The priest says "Amen" and stands upright. The acolyte then repeats the Confiteor in the name of all present, with appropriate changes.

WHAT a solemn moment! In the presence of the holy, omniscient God, both priest and people feel their guilt and publicly ask for grace and pardon. The soul must cleanse itself in the waters of contrition at the very beginning of this sublime act. How could it otherwise receive the full benefits of the approaching Mystery?

As once on the Cross Our Lord took upon Himself the sins of the whole world, to atone for them with His Blood, so now we lay our sins upon Him as upon a victim about to be immolated on the altar, that He may expiate them. It is to indicate this that the priest at the commencement of the Mass bows down at the foot of the altar, and in the spirit of humility presents himself as if laden with the sins of the people before the Eternal Father, in order to prevail upon Him to have mercy. In this position he also personifies Christ upon the Mount of Olives, who, bowed down under the burden of the sins of the whole world, fell upon His face. His sweat becoming as drops of blood, and prayed earnestly to His Heavenly Father. In like manner, Christ's representative prays for the pardon of his own sins and the sins of all present, for whom the price of Redemption was once paid, and is daily offered anew to operate the remission of sin.

No sooner has the priest heard the faithful, in their turn, acknowledging their sins, than he invokes a blessing upon them:—

℣. *Misereatur vestri omnipotens Deus, et, dimissis peccatis vestris, perducat vos ad vitam arternam.*
℟. *Amen.*

May Almighty God have mercy upon you, forgive you your sins, and bring you to life everlasting.
℟. Amen.

Signing himself with the Sign of the Cross, the priest continues:—

Indulgentiam, absolutionem et remissionem peccatorum nostrorum, tribuat nobis omnipotens et misericors Dominus. ℟. *Amen.*

May the almighty and merciful Lord grant us pardon, absolution, and remission of our sins. ℟. Amen.

The priest stands erect after his previous humble posture, to signify by this upright position that both he and the faithful are uplifted and comforted by the firm hope of receiving the forgiveness of their sins. Consolation now fills the heart of the priest, and bowing, he turns to God with these trustful words upon his lips:—

℣. *Deus, tu conversis vivificabis nos.*
℟. *Et plebs tua laetabitur in te.*

℣. *Ostende nobis, Domine, misericordiam tuam.*
℟. *Et salutare tuum da nobis.*
℣. *Domine exaudi orationem meam.*
℟. *Et clamor meus ad te veniat.*

℣. *Dominus vobiscum.*
℟. *Et cum spiritu tuo.*

℣. Thou shalt turn again, O God, and quicken us.
℟. And Thy people shall rejoice in Thee.

℣. Show unto us, O Lord, Thy mercy.
℟. And grant us Thy salvation.
℣. O Lord, hear my prayer.
℟. And let my cry come unto Thee.

℣. The Lord be with you.
℟. And with thy spirit.

Extending and then joining his hands, the priest says, "Oremus—Let us Pray."

The word *Oremus* introduces nearly all the liturgical prayers. It implies an invitation to those present to join with the priest in presenting the petitions of the faithful in the name of Holy Mother Church, rather than to pursue their private devotions.

At the Altar

HANDS which touch things sacred can never be sufficiently pure, nor can souls called by God to the sublime dignity of the priesthood ever be sufficiently innocent. Conscious of this fact, the priest, although he has just implored pardon of his sins and has heard from the faithful a heartfelt *Misereatur,* still feels keenly his need of Divine mercy. Therefore, as he ascends the altar steps, he implores the Lord to look with kindness upon him and upon all present, to grant them pardon, and to lend a merciful ear to the silent yet mighty cry of the hearts of the faithful: —

Aufer a nobis, quaesumus, Domine, iniquitates nostras: ut ad Sancta sanectorum puris mereamur mentibus introire. Per Christum Dominum nostrum. Amen.	Take away from us our iniquities, we beseech Thee, O Lord, that we may be made worthy to enter with pure minds into the holy of holies. Through Christ our Lord. Amen.

Will God hear his prayer? Of this the priest cannot be certain; therefore he calls upon the saints, the friends of God, to intercede for him with the Almighty. Bowing low over the altar, he kisses the altar stone which encloses the relics of the saints, while he prays: —

Oramus te, Domine, per merita Sanctorum tuorum, quorum reliquiae hic sunt, et omnium Sanctorum, ut indulgere digneris omnia peccata mea. Amen.	We beseech Thee, O Lord, by the merits of Thy saints whose relics are here and of all the saints, that Thou wouldst vouchsafe to forgive me all my sins. Amen.

In the beautiful language of symbolism, this kiss is expressive also of a greeting to Christ, the Bridegroom, who is represented by the altar, on the part of His Bride, the Church.

The priest then goes to the Epistle side of the altar, makes the Sign of the Cross and recites the

Introit

THE *Introit* is a verse from the Psalms or the Old Testament and varies according to the feast celebrated or the season of the year. It stands in close relationship with, and is, so to say, the *key* to a right understanding of the Epistle and Gospel. It expresses the spirit of the feast or the mystery being celebrated—whether of joy, of gratitude, of hope, of longing, of desire, of petition—and the sentiments which ought principally to animate the hearts of the faithful.

On the feasts of saints, the *Introit* recalls the vocation, the outstanding work, the sufferings, the glorification, etc. of the saint who is being honored. On the various Sundays of the year, the *Introit* announces some truth of religion, or a Divine promise, or recalls some event which inspires confidence, reverence, resignation, or some other virtue. Sometimes it is a plea for help or for mercy, or again, an invitation to give praise and thanks to God.

During Advent we cry with ardent longing for the Redeemer in the words of Isaias, "Drop down dew, ye heavens, from above, and let the clouds rain the just: let the earth be opened, and bud forth a Savior" (Isaias 45: 8). At Christmas we rejoice in the birth of the "Prince of Peace." In the *Introit* of the Mass of Corpus Christi we rejoice in the great gift of the Holy Eucharist, the Heavenly Bread with which we are fed.

Cibavit eos ex adipe frumenti, alleluia; et de petra melle saturavit eos, alleluia, alleluia, alleluia. ℟. *Exultate Deo adjutori nostro; jubilate Deo Jacob,* ℣. *Gloria.*	He fed them with the fat of wheat, alleluia; and filled them with honey out of the rock, alleluia, alleluia, alleluia. ℟. Rejoice in God our helper; sing aloud to the God of Jacob. ℣. Glory.

Kyrie

With sentiments of complete dependence on God, the priest, returning to the center of the altar, with hands joined before his breast, implores mercy for himself and the people, repeating alternately with the server, the words: "Kyrie eleison, Christe eleison, Kyrie eleison," each invocation being repeated three times.

Holy Church, the Mystical Bride of Christ, sends heavenward her pilgrim-song of exile—the Kyrie eleison.

THE words *Kyrie eleison* are taken from the Greek language and mean "Lord, have mercy on us." Though the prayers of the Mass are in Latin, these Greek words, as also "Amen," "Alleluia" and "Hosanna" taken from the Hebrew, are retained. This threefold petition to each Person of the Holy Trinity is expressive of the earnestness with which we implore the Divine mercy. We call upon the Father to be merciful to us through His omnipotence; upon the Son, to be merciful to us through His wisdom; and upon the Holy Ghost, to be merciful to us through His goodness. We implore mercy because we have often offended, the Heavenly Father, who in His power has created us; because we have often offended the Eternal Son, who through His wisdom has endured such great sufferings to redeem us; because we have often offended the Holy Spirit, who through His goodness has sanctified us.

Mercy is one of the most touching attributes of God. Our creation, our redemption and our sanctification are effects of God's mercy. We need not fear to ask for great mercies; the more He gives the more glory He receives. His mercy is as a great and boundless ocean which envelops us; we need but reach out to draw therefrom. It is true, God's justice demands its rights, but precisely on account of His justice God will be merciful to those who implore mercy, because of justice to His only-begotten Son, who has paid so great a price to obtain mercy for us.

The psalmist cries out: "Thou, O Lord, art sweet and mild: and plenteous in mercy to all that call upon Thee" (Ps. 85: 5). God desires to give; He loves to be entreated to give; it is His nature to be ever giving; and regarding man it has been said: "There is nothing more Godlike than to give." The mercy of God is infinite.

We take into consideration far too little the essence of God. We forget that with Him nothing may be measured by our standards. He loves us in an infinite degree. We must be convinced of this, after all He has done for us. The damned will regret nothing so much as not to have benefited by the goodness and mercy of God.

As Jesus Christ suffered so inexpressibly much for us and shed His Blood even to the last drop, is it not meet that the power and efficacy of this Blood should come to Its just rights wherever and whenever the hand of man reaches out for It? Consider the penitent thief on the cross. We, too, speak words imploring mercy at Holy Mass. The words are short— "Lord, have mercy on us; Christ, have mercy on us; Lord, have mercy on us." With God our words are not counted but weighed. May these words, Kyrie eleison, ever come forth from our heart as a burning petition for mercy from the Triune God.

Joy in God

GLORIA[3]

Having said the last "Kyrie," the priest standing in the same place extends his hands, raises them, and intones the "Gloria, in excelsis Deo." At the word "Deo" he joins his hands, and bows his head to the Crucifix; then, standing erect, he continues the "Gloria." to the end with hands joined, bowing his head when he says: "Adoramus te; Gratias agimus tibi; Jesu Christi; Suscipe deprecationem nostram." At the end, he makes the Sign of the Cross on himself when he says: "Cum Sancto Spiritu."

Gloria in excelsis Deo. Et in terra pax hominibus bonae voluntatis. Laudamus te. Benedicimus te. Adoramus te. Glorificamus te. Gratias agimus tibi propter magnam gloriam tuam. Domine Deus Rex caelestis, Deus Pater omnipotens. Domine Fili unigenite, Jesu Christe. Domine Deus, Agnus Dei, Filius Patris. Qui tollis peccata mundi, miserere nobis. Qui tollis peccata mundi, suscipe deprecationem nostram.

Glory be to God on high, and on earth peace to men of good will. We praise Thee; we bless Thee; we adore Thee; we glorify Thee. We give Thee thanks for Thy great glory, O Lord God, Heavenly King, God the Father Almighty. O Lord Jesus Christ, the only-begotten Son: O Lord God, Lamb of God, Son of the Father, who takest away the sins of the world have mercy on us; who takest away the sins of the world,

---

[3] *The "Gloria," being a hymn of praise, is omitted in Masses for the dead, during the seasons of Advent and Lent, and also on other occasions when the expression of joy is inappropriate.*

Joy in God

Qui sedes ad dexteram Patris, miserere nobis. Quoniam tu solus sanctus. Tu solus Dominus. Tu solus altissimus, Jesu Christe. Cum Sancto Spiritu, in gloria Dei Patris. Amen.

receive our prayer: who sittest at the right hand of the Father, have mercy on us. For Thou only are holy: Thou only art the Lord: Thou only, O Jesus Christ, art most high, together with the Holy Ghost, in the glory of God the Father. Amen.

TRULY, this is a prayer of "joy in God." It is an expression of gratitude and joy for our Redemption, which is renewed in every Holy Mass. Holy Church borrows from the angels the canticle of joy which they sang above the manger of the Infant God and adds to it her own expressions of gratitude and praise. As the angels intoned this canticle when the great work of our Redemption began in Bethlehem, so we echo their song as we are preparing to celebrate the renewal of the Redemption in Holy Mass and to offer the sublime Sacrifice of praise and thanksgiving.

Our hearts overflow with gratitude for the benefits of the incarnation, and we voice our thanksgiving in these fervent exclamations: — *Laudamus te, benedicimus te, adoramus te, glorificamus te!* Whenever we wish to give expression to our praise of God, these words are most beautiful to repeat: "We praise Thee, we bless Thee, we adore Thee, we glorify Thee!" We also thank God for His glory, for we and all things have been created for His glory. What a sublime thought: To thank God—not for His benefits to man,—creation, redemption, the promise of heaven—but to thank Him for His own glory—to think only of God and His attributes!

After we have praised God for His great glory, we turn to the Eternal Son enthroned at the right hand of the Father, and call upon His mercy and goodness. We behold in our Savior the Lamb of God immolated for the sins of the world. We implore Him to take away our sins and to receive our prayer. We plead with Him in the oft-repeated cry of the liturgy, in virtue of His power—"Who sittest at the right hand of the Father"—to have mercy on us. We praise and extol Him as the highest King and Lord who lives and reigns from eternity to eternity and who will prepare a throne for us near His own, He who is one with the Holy Ghost in unending glory.

The *Gloria* is a sublime hymn of praise, and we should repeat it in the spirit of a joyful welcome to our Savior who is soon to be born anew upon the altar as He was born in the cave at Bethlehem. Jesus is present in the Most Blessed Sacrament as truly as He was in the grotto. The tabernacle is as the stable of His Eucharistic life, the ciborium as His manger, the white form of the Sacred Host as His swathing bands. Here, too, He is often exposed to bitter cold; it is winter about Him because many times He is surrounded by the cold blasts of the indifference and ingratitude of the hearts of men. Let us join with the angels in praising Him, with the shepherds in adoring Him, with the Magi in glorifying Him.

Dominus Vobiscum

When the "Gloria" is ended, the priest turns to the people, extends his arms and says:

℣. *Dominus vobiscum.* ℣. The Lord be with you.

FREQUENTLY during Holy Mass the priest salutes the congregation with these words, *Dominus vobiscum.* This is an ancient form of greeting, expressive of everything good, for whosoever has the Lord with him wants nothing. These words express the wish of the priest in behalf of the faithful who are present, that God may be with them and assist them to pray in spirit and in truth, for special grace is needed in order to pray well. We need the Divine assistance in order that our petitions may be offered for the things that are best and may find a ready hearing at the throne of Divine Mercy.

The congregation answers, through the server:

℞. *Et cum spiritu tuo.*   And with thy spirit.

It is as though the faithful were to say: "May the Lord be with thy spirit, O Shepherd of our souls, for thou prayest for us and teachest us the way of life eternal; therefore does thy spirit need the Lord to be near." This versicle and response, repeated so often, during Mass, signify the close relation that exists between the priest and the people. When the priest says *Dominus vobiscum*, he extends his arms and hands toward the people as a sign of reverent affection, and to indicate a blessing.

COLLECT

The celebrant then goes to the right of the altar and inclines toward the Crucifix.

WITH the words, "*Oremus*—Let us pray," the priest invites the congregation to join him in his supplication, indicating by these words the union of his heart with theirs. Then follow the *Collects*, or collective prayers for the day, which for conciseness of form, richness of expression and depth of meaning, have never been equaled. They are called "collective" prayers because they sum up all the intentions and needs of the Church and of her children, both spiritual and temporal, which are laid before God by the priest. The priest extends his hands and then folds them as a mark of humility, acknowledging that we can do nothing of our own strength and that we must put all our trust in

God. Afterwards he extends them once more in an attitude of appeal in memory of our Savior who, with arms extended upon the Cross, interceded with His Heavenly Father for the whole human race.

Nearly all these prayers[4] conclude with the words, "Per Dominum nostrum Jesum Christum—Through Jesus Christ our Lord..." for the Heavenly Father has given us the promise that He will refuse nothing which we ask in the Name of His beloved Son, Jesus.

At these words the priest again joins his hands. The server answers — in the name of the people—"*Amen*—So be it," by these words sealing the petitions which have been uttered by the priest.

Every *Collect* may be divided into three parts: first, the *invocation*; second, the *subject*, or matter which we desire by the prayer; and third, the *pleading* through the merits of our Lord and Savior that we may obtain what we ask. Take, for example, the Collects for the festival of Corpus Christi:

Deus, qui nobis sub Sacramento mirabili passionis tuae memoriam reliquisti: tribue, quaesumus; ita nos Corporis et Sanguinis tui sacra mysteria venerari, ut redemptionis tuae fructum in nobis jugiter sentiamus. Qui vivis et regnas...	O God, who in this wonderful Sacrament hast left us a memorial of Thy Passion: grant us, we beseech Thee, so to venerate the sacred mysteries of Thy Body and Blood, that we may ever feel within us the fruit of Thy Redemption. Who livest and reignest.

The first part of this prayer is an *invocation*, a calling upon God. Then follows the *petition*, beseeching Christ that we may venerate the Most Blessed Sacrament in such a manner

---

[4] *Most of the* Collect *prayers are addressed to the Triune God. The* Collect *for the festival of Corpus Christi is one of the few exceptions, as it is addressed directly to our Lord Jesus Christ Himself, and therefore, the wording at the end is not the usual formula, "through Jesus Christ, our Lord."*

as to profit by Its fruits for our Redemption; and lastly we pray that this grace may be granted by His merits.

Sometimes there are several *Collects* added to the *Collect* of the day. These are either commemorations of saints, whose feast occurs on that day, or of the Blessed Virgin, or prayers for various occasions and necessities. Whenever the Most Blessed Sacrament is exposed, no matter what *Collect* is said for the season or for the feast, the *Collect of the Blessed Sacrament* must also be said. There are but a few exceptions to this rule, namely when the Holy Mass is in honor of the Sacred Heart, the Most Precious Blood, the Passion, the Holy Cross, or the Most Holy Redeemer.

Heralds Prepare the Way

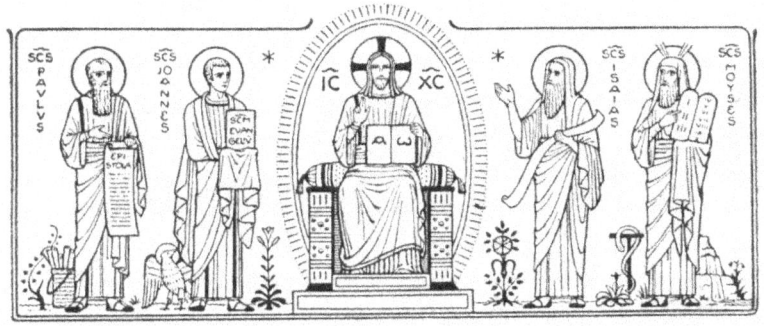

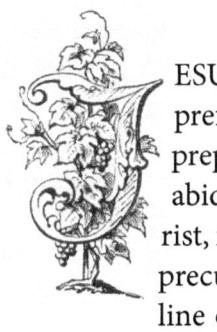

ESUS Christ was announced by the prophets and prefigured by numerous types in the Old Law to prepare the people for His coming. Now that He abides with us under the appearances of the Eucharist, it is the same. At every Holy Mass He sends His precursor before Him to prepare the way. The great line of patriarchs and prophets has been increased by the apostles and evangelists. All these great men of God were heralds of the Almighty. They spoke of a God, a Man, a Redeemer, a King of heaven and earth, a Lawgiver, a Judge and a Recompenser. They made known His commands, His promises, His threats. They also portrayed His life and death.

The office of teaching likewise constitutes an essential part of the sublime Sacrifice of Redemption. The Epistle and Gospel represent to us the teaching of Christ; portions of Holy Scripture, proper to the feast or season, are chosen for each day. The Epistle unfolds to us the indirect teaching of the Redeemer, as transmitted through the patriarchs, prophets and Apostles. This teaching should prepare the heart and lead it to Christ, who speaks to it Himself in the holy Gospel. For this reason the Epistle precedes the Gospel.

Epistle

IN THE first ages of Christianity, passages from the prophets were read before the holy Gospel; later, also passages from the letters of the Apostles. In the Roman liturgy, the Epistle varies. It is taken from the Old or from the New Testament, and the lessons are more frequently taken from the letters of the Apostles than from the prophets. Therefore, we call the Lesson "Epistle," which means "letter." Formerly the Epistle was read by the lector from a special elevated place, a kind of pulpit; since the eighth century, the Epistle is read by the subdeacon at Solemn High Mass, and at the ordinary celebration of Mass, the priest himself reads it. Formerly, the celebrating bishop or priest decided what was to be read each time. The present order of the Epistles and Gospels was arranged by St. Jerome (died 420) and finally established by Pope St. Pius V, in 1570.

The priest lays his hand upon the book or altar while reading the Epistle, to show us that we should be ready at once to put our hand to the work in order to conform our life to the principles laid down for us in the Epistle.

What a wealth of instruction and what an unerring guide for our conduct is given to us by St. Paul in the Epistle for the feast of Corpus Christi: —

Fratres, Ego enim accepi a Domino quod et tradidi vobis, quoniam Dominus Jesus, in qua nocte tradebatur, accepit panem, et gratias agens fregit, et dixit: Accipite, et manducate: hoc est Corpus meum quod pro vobis tradetur: hoc facite in meam commemorationem. Similiter et calicem, postquam coenavit, dicens: Hic calix novum Testamentum est in meo Sanguine. Hoc facite, quotiescumque bibetis, in meam commemorationem. Quotiescumque enim manducabitis panem hunc, et calicem bibetis, mortem Domini, annuntiabitis donec veniat. Itaque: quicumque manducaverit panem hunc, vel biberit calicem Domini indigne, reus erit Corporis et Sanguinis Domini. Probet autem seipsum homo, et sic de pane illo edat, et de calice bibat. Qui enim manducat et bibit indigne, judicium sibi manducat et bibit, non dijudicans Corpus Domini (1 Cor. 11: 23-30).

Brethren: I myself have received from the Lord (what I also delivered to you), that the Lord Jesus, on the night in which He was betrayed, took bread, and giving thanks broke, and said, "This is My Body which shall be given up for you; do this in remembrance of Me." In like manner also the Cup, after He had supped, saying, "This Cup is the new covenant in My Blood; do this as often as you drink it, in remembrance of Me. For as often as you shall eat this Bread and drink of the Cup, you proclaim the Death of the Lord, until He comes." Therefore whoever eats this Bread or drinks the Cup of the Lord unworthily, will be guilty of the Body and the Blood of the Lord. But let a man prove himself, and so let him eat of that Bread and drink of the Cup; for he who eats and drinks unworthily, without distinguishing the Body, eats and drinks judgment to himself. (1 Cor. 11; 23-30).

At the conclusion of the Epistle, the server answers, in the name of the people, *"Deo gratias! —*Thanks be to God!" in order to express their gratitude for the Divine revelation, which God does not grant to everyone. Willingness to fulfill God's precepts, and gratitude for His sacred Word are the sentiments which should animate the Christian during the *Epistle* and the *Gradual* which immediately follows it.

Gradual

The priest, remaining in the same position as at the Epistle, now reads the "Gradual."

THE *Gradual* formerly consisted of an entire psalm or psalms and was sung with great solemnity. It is so called because it used to be sung from the steps (gradus) of the altar or pulpit. Pope Gregory the Great (died 604) reduced the length of the psalm to the present few verses which epitomize the *Epistle*. These few verses are so appropriately selected that they are little masterpieces, both from a literary and a spiritual standpoint. Like a golden thread, the spirit of the Mass is woven through the *Collect, Epistle,* and *Gradual,* showing the completeness and the exceedingly beautiful arrangement of the liturgy. The *Gradual* expresses the sentiments and dispositions which the *Epistle* should produce in our souls.

For instance, in the Mass of Corpus Christi we honor the Most Blessed Sacrament as the memorial of the Passion, and in the *Collect* we ask that through the sacred mysteries of Christ's Body and Blood we may feel within us the fruit of the Redemption. St. Paul speaks to us in the Epistle, exhorting us to receive the most sacred Body and Blood of the Lord worthily. The *Gradual,* after exciting us to trust in God's Providence and gratitude for His benefits, ends with those beautiful words of Our Lord which tell us of our inestimable privilege and dignity of being united with Jesus Christ through the Holy Eucharist:

Oculi omnium in te sperant, Domine: et tu das illis escam in tempore opportuno. ℣. Aperis tu manum tuam, et imples omne animal benedictione. Alleluia, alleluia. ℣. Caro mea vere est cibus, et Sanguis meus vere est potus: qui manducat meam Carnem, et bibit meum Sanguinem, in me manet, et ego in eo (John 6).

The eyes of all hope in Thee, O Lord, and Thou givest them meat in due season. ℣. Thou openest Thy hand, and fillest every living creature with Thy blessings. Alleluia, alleluia. ℣. My Flesh is meat indeed, and My Blood is drink indeed: he that eateth My Flesh and drinketh My Blood abideth in Me, and I in him *(John 6).*

The *Gradual* changes according to the feasts and the different seasons of the year. It is omitted during Paschal time, and two other verses are said in its place. Like the *Introit,* the *Gradual* verses announce the purpose for which the Mass is being said; —whether it be in honor of some saint, of some mystery of our holy religion, for the departed, or for some other intention.

In times of joy and special solemnity, two *Alleluias* with a verse followed by a third *Alleluia,* are added to the *Gradual. Alleluia* is a Hebrew word which means "Praise the Lord." As it expresses a transport of joy which cannot be adequately rendered by any term in Greek or Latin, it has been retained in its original form.

TRACT AND SEQUENCE

IN times of penance and sorrow the *Alleluias* would be out of place. They are, therefore, omitted on such occasions, together with the versicle, and other verses are substituted. These latter verses, taken from the psalms or the Old Testament, form what is called the *Tract.*

On certain days, when Holy Church wishes to prolong the joy of the *Alleluia* or the sorrow and expression of penance in the *Tract,* she adds a hymn or psalm called the *Sequence.* There are now five Sequences in our Missal, as follows: —

Victimae Paschali for Easter Sunday, supposed to have been composed by a priest named Wipo about 1048.

Veni Sancte Spiritus for Pentecost, ascribed to Pope Innocent III about 1198.

Lauda Sion for Corpus Christi, composed by St. Thomas Aquinas about 1274.

Stabat Mater for the Feast of the Sorrowful Mother, generally attributed to a Franciscan friar; composed about 1306.

Dies Irae, in Masses for the Departed, also believed to have been composed by a Franciscan friar about 1250.

These *Sequences* abound in poetic beauty, depth of thought and doctrinal soundness, as we will fully realize by reading attentively the incomparable *Sequence* for the feast of Corpus Christi. On account of its length, we give only the English translation here.

Sion, lift thy voice and sing,
Praise thy Savior, praise thy King;
Praise with hymns thy Shepherd true:
Strive thy best to praise Him well,
For He doth all praise excel;
None can ever reach His due.

See today before us laid
Living and life-giving Bread,
Theme for praise and joy profound;
Bread which at the sacred board
Was, by our Incarnate Lord,
Giv'n to His Apostles round.

Let the praise be loud and high;
Sweet and rev'rent be the joy
Felt today in every breast;
On this festival Divine,
Which records the orgin
Of the glorious Eucharist.

On this table of the new King,
This, the New Law's paschal off'ring
Brings to end the olden rite.
Here, for empty shadows fled,
Is reality instead;
Here, instead of darkness light.

What He did at supper seated
Christ ordained to be repeated,
In His memory Divine;
Wherefore we, with adoration
Thus the Host of our salvation
Consecrate from bread and wine.

Taught by Christ, the Church maintaineth,
That the bread its substance changeth
Into Flesh, the wine to Blood.
Doth it pass thy comprehending?
Faith, the law of sight transcending
Leaps to things not understood.

Here, beneath these signs, are hidden
Priceless things, to sense forbidden.
Signs, not things, are all we see, —
Flesh from bread, and Blood from
    wine.
Yet is Christ in either sign,
All entire, confessed to be.

They, too, who of Him partake,
Sever not, nor rend, nor break,
But entire, their Lord receive,
Whether one or thousands eat,
All receive the selfsame meat,
Nor the less for others leave.

Lo, the wicked with the good
Eat of this celestial food:
Yet with ends how opposite!
Life to these, 'tis death to those:
See how form like taking flows
Diff'rence truly infinite.

Nor do though doubts entertain
When the Host is broken in twain:
But be sure, each part contains
What was in the whole before;

'Tis the simple sign alone
Which hath changed in size and
    form.
While the signified is one
And the same for evermore.

Lo, upon the alter lies,
Hidden deep from human eyes,
Bread of angels from the skies,
Made the food of mortal man:
Children's meat, to dogs denied;
In old types foresignified:
In the manna heaven supplied,
Isaac, and the Paschal Lamb.

Jesu, Shepherd, Bread indeed,
Thou take pity on our need:
Thou Thy flock in safety feed,
Thou protect us, Thou us lead
To the land of heavenly grace.
Thou, who feedest us below,
Source of all we have or know,
Grant that, at Thy feast of love,
Sitting with the saints above,
We may see Thee face to face.
    Amen. Alleluia.

Gospel

Having read the Epistle and the prayers which follow, the priest leaves the Missal open and goes to the center of the altar, where, raising his eyes to the Crucifix, and immediately lowering them again, he inclines profoundly, keeping his hands joined. Meanwhile the acolyte goes up to the altar, takes the Missal from the Epistle side, descends to the foot of the steps, genuflects, and takes it up to the left or Gospel side.

THE priest is about to read the holy Gospel, but out of reverence for its sacred words, he first stands with bowed head before the center of the altar and prays:

Munda cor meum, ac labia mea, omnipotens Deus, qui labia Isaiae Prophetae calculo mundasti ignito: ita me tuo grata miseratione dignare mundare, ut sanctum Evangelium tuum digne valeam nuntiare. Per Christum Dominum nostrum. Amen.	Cleanse my heart and my lips, O God Almighty, who didst cleanse the lips of the Prophet Isaias[5] with a burning coal; and vouchsafe through Thy gracious mercy, so, to purify me that I may worthily proclaim Thy holy Gospel. Through Christ our Lord. Amen.
Jube, Domine, benedicere. Dominus sit in corde meo et in labiis meis, ut digne et competenter annuntiem Evangelium suum. Amen.	Pray, Lord, a blessing. The Lord be in my heart and on my lips, that I may worthily and in a becoming manner announce His holy Gospel. Amen.

Well may the priest ask that his lips be cleansed, because he is about to proclaim the words of Christ which are great in their holiness, great in their wisdom, and great in their power. From the Divine lips came, in a few clear, significant words, the truest, the most exalted, the most practical doctrine concerning God and heavenly things, concerning man and his destiny, concerning the world and its filial dissolution. The speech of Jesus is full of beauty; His words are luminous, "enlightening every man that cometh into this world" (John 1: 9). His words are powerful and convincing when He teaches those truths which the greatest and most devout intellects have studied uninterruptedly for over nineteen hundred years without fully comprehending; and which other great but impious minds of all ages have not yet been able to overthrow, despite all their painstaking efforts. His words are strong and terrible, thundering against the profaners of the temple and against the deceitful Pharisees. His words are most touching, especially when, at the Last Supper He gives the final pledges of His love and bids His Apostles a last farewell. His words are inimitable, whether He teaches or condemns, whether He prays or mourns. His words distill a heavenly unction; they bear the stamp of Divinity.

The Missal is carried from the Epistle to the Gospel side of the altar to indicate that the light of Faith, having been rejected by the Jews, was carried to the Gentiles. No book should be preferred to the book of the holy Gospel. With the deepest reverence, with a holy timidity and a heart overflowing with gratitude should we read these living words of Jesus Christ.

Having prayed that his lips be purified, the priest stands erect and with hands joined goes to the Gospel side and says:

℣. *Dominus vobiscum.*
℟. *Et cum spiritu tuo.*

℣. ℟. The Lord be with you.
℟. And with thy spirit.

℣. *Sequentia* (sive *Initium*) *sancti Evangelii secundum N .*
℟. *Gloria tibi, Domine.*

℣. The *continuation* (or *beginning*) of the holy Gospel according to N.
℟. Glory be to Thee, O Lord.

The priest makes the Sign of the Cross on the book at the beginning of the Gospel, then on his forehead, lips and breast. This is a prayer that the holy Gospel may be, first, in our mind, that we may know Our Lord's teachings; secondly, on our lips, that we may fearlessly proclaim the truths of our holy Faith, thirdly, in our heart, that we may faithfully live according to the precepts of the holy Gospel. The faithful also rise, to express their readiness to follow the teachings contained in our Savior's words.

In the Gospel, Christ speaks directly to each one of us. The parables and examples He shows us contain, lessons for our daily life. They tell us of His love, mercy, gentleness, patience, long-suffering and charity. Every action, every word, has its special meaning. How sublime and majestic are His words as He announces the Mystery of the Holy Eucharist, in which all the laws of nature are set aside to make way for the law of His infinite love:

In illo tempore: Dixit Jesus turbis Judaeorum: Caro mea vere est cibus, et Sanguis meus vere est potus. Qui manducat meam Carnem, et bibit meum Sanguinem, in me manet, et ego in illo. Sicut misit me vivens Pater, et ego vivo propter Patrem: et qui manducat me, et ipse vivet propter me. Hic est panis qui de caelo descendit. Non sicut manducaverunt patres vestri manna, et mortui sunt. Qui manducat hunc panem, vivet in aeternum.	At that time: Jesus said to the multitude of the Jews: "My Flesh is food indeed and My Blood is drink indeed. He who eats My Flesh, and drinks My Blood, abides in Me and I in him. As the living Father has sent Me, and as I live because of the Father, so he who eats Me, he also shall live because of Me. This is the Bread that has come down from heaven; not as your fathers ate the manna, and died. He who eats this Bread shall live forever" (John 6: 56-59).

The faithful answer, through the server: "*Laus tibi Christe*— Praise be to Thee, O Christ!" as an expression of their gratitude for the teachings of Our Lord contained in the Gospel, and as an act of thanksgiving to Jesus Christ who Himself brought us the glad tidings of Redemption and God's kingdom. When the Gospel is finished, the priest raises the Missal, with both hands, inclines a little, and kisses it where he signed it at the beginning, to show his love and veneration for the Divine word.[5] While kissing the Gospel, the priest says, in a low voice: "*Per evangelica dicta deleantur nostra delicta*—By the words of the Gospel may our sins be blotted out." The words of the Gospel, attentively and devoutly received, impart grace which leads to contrition and confession for the cleansing of our sins.

The moment when our Savior is to be in our midst, draws ever nearer. The Church wishes, before she gives our Redeemer to us, to show us, through the holy Gospel, who Jesus is, what He has done for us, and what He expects of us.

---

[5] *In Masses for the Departed,* Munda cor meum *is said, but a blessing is not asked, nor does the priest kiss the book.*

This is usually explained to the faithful by Christ's minister who on Sundays and holy days delivers a sermon after the Gospel.

The Torch of Faith

Nicene Creed

WE HAVE heard proclaimed the joyous Gospel tidings. We have read from the book of life. The Divine Teacher has Himself instructed us by His powerful words, His heavenly words, His grace-giving words. He has told us that He came to seek and to save. He has exhorted us to carry our cross after Him if we wish to be His disciples. He has given proofs of His goodness and love. He has told us of the beauty of heaven and the reward awaiting those who strive to attain it. Still under the wondrous spell of His great miracles, His sublime teaching and His Divine example, the Catholic heart with joy cries out:

Credo in unum Deum, Patrem omnipotentem, factorem coeli et terrae, visibilium omnium, et invisibilium. Et in unum Dominum Jesum Christum, Filium Dei unigenitum: et ex Patre natum ante omnia saecula, Deum de Deo, lumen de lumine, Deum verum de Deo vero; genitum, non factum, consubstantialem Patri; per quem omnia facta sunt. Qui propter nos homines, et propter nostram salutem, descendit de coelis (hic genuflectitur). *Et incarnatus est de Spiritu sancto ex Maria Virgine:* et homo factus est. *Crucifixus etiam pro nobis: sub Pontio Pilato passus et sepultus est. Et resurrexit tertia die, secundum Scripturas. Et ascendit in coelum, sedet ad dexteram Patris. Et iterum venturus est cum gloria judicare vivos et mortuos: cujus regni non erit finis. Et in Spiritum sanctum Dominum et vivificantem, qui ex Patre Filioque procedit. Qui cum Patre et Filio simul adoratur et conglorificatur; qui locutus est per prophetas. Et unam, sanctam, catholicam et apostolicam Ecclesiam. Confiteor unum baptisma in remissionem peccatorum. Et exspecto resurrectionem mortuorum, et vitam venturi saeculi. Amen.*

I believe in one God, the Father Almighty, maker of heaven and earth, and all things visible and invisible. And in one Lord Jesus Christ, the only-begotten Son of God, born of the Father before all ages; God of God, light of light, true God of true God; begotten not made; consubstantial with the Father; by whom all things were made. Who for us men, and for our salvation, came down from heaven *(here all kneel);* and was incarnate by the Holy Ghost, of the Virgin Mary; and *was made man.* He was crucified also for us, suffered under Pontius Pilate and was buried. And the third day He rose again according to the Scriptures; and ascended into heaven. He sitteth at the right hand of the Father, and He shall come again with glory to judge the living and the dead; and His kingdom shall have no end. And in the Holy Ghost, the Lord and giver of life, who pro-ceedeth from the Father and the Son, who together with the Father and the Son, is adored and glorified; who spoke by the prophets. And one, holy, catholic and apostolic Church. I confess one baptism for the remission of sins. And I await the resurrection of the dead, and the life of the world to come. Amen.

"*Credo*—I believe!" Glorious word! How impressive it sounds at this moment when the Savior is nigh. He will soon be on the altar. With the greatest ardor we should long for His coming. There is no more appropriate time than now to pour forth to Jesus the beautiful profession of our faith. Truly, the faithful soul must of necessity break forth in jubilation: "My Lord, and my God, I believe in Thee, I believe in Thy word, and in this faith I will live and die."

THE SUBSTANCE OF OUR BELIEF

> The priest, standing at the middle of the altar, extends, elevates and then joins his hands while he says the "Nicene Creed." When he says, "Deum" he bows his head to the Crucifix, as also at the words "Jesum Christum" and "simul adoratur." When uttering the words: "Et incarnatus est—and was made Flesh," he genuflects on one knee until after the words: "Et homo factus est—and was made man." As he says the last words of the "Credo," he makes the Sign of the Cross. At the word "Amen" he places his hands on the altar.

LET us, too, with holy fervor, bend our knee at the words: *Et incarnatus est*. Let us worship our Divine Savior in the spirit of the shepherds and the Magi, when they adored Him in the crib at Bethlehem. If Christ had not become incarnate, there would be no Creed, no Holy Catholic Church; there would be no hope for us of forgiveness of sins or the glory of heaven to come. The Creed contains the whole substance of our Catholic belief.

Our Lord in all His mysteries can be placed before us under four titles: (1) As our great *God*; (2) as our loving *Brother*; (3) as our *Oblation*; (4) as our *Bridegroom*. He is presented to us under these four aspects in the Creed. (1) We acknowledge that He is *true God* of *true God*; (2) that He made Himself our *Brother* by taking our human flesh with all the affections of a human heart; (3) that He suffered and died for us, thus becoming our Sacrifice, our *Oblation*; (4) that He is our glorious *Bridegroom*, who "on the third day arose again from the dead, ascended into heaven, sitteth at the right hand of God the Father Almighty, from thence He shall come to judge the living and the dead." In these sentences of the Creed, the whole adorable Person of Christ is presented to us. We review the mystery of His life, starting from the highest throne in heaven where He is and always has been adored eternally; then we follow Him to the abasement of His incarnation; next, to the sufferings of His bitter Passion, and Death, and finally back to His glory in heaven, with the hope of one day rising with Him to everlasting life.

The Fruit of the Gospel

THE Nicene Creed is the confession of faith as it was formulated at the first general Council of Nice (325) and developed at the Council of Constantinople (381). It was prayed at Holy Mass in all the Eastern churches from about the middle of the fifth century. In the churches of the West it was not introduced until some time later. The Creed marks the end of the "Mass of the Catechumens," or the first part of the Holy Sacrifice. It is placed at the end of the prophetic part of Holy Mass and constitutes, as it were, the *fruit of the Gospel*. The Creed is, at the same time, a fitting transition to the second part of Holy Mass, the true sacrifice. The true love of sacrifice springs from a living faith; therefore those present once more re-animate their faith so that they may with fervor take part in the sacrifice itself. The Creed is not always said at Mass, but only on certain days. The days on which it is to be said are arranged in the liturgy according to mystery, doctrine, and celebration or solemnity. By reason of the mysteries of our religion, it is to be said on all the festivals of Our Lord and His Blessed Mother; by reason of the doctrines of faith, it is to be said on all the feasts of the Apostles and Doctors of the Church; and by reason of celebration or solemnity, it is to be said on the feasts of patrons and other feasts of the first and second class, when the people are supposed to attend Mass in greater number. It is also said during the octaves of greater feasts.

Sentiments of gratitude should fill our hearts while we sing or pray the Creed. Too often we say it thoughtlessly, without realizing that it is something holy, something sublime, which the Church has preserved for us down through the centuries, and which sets forth the same truths which the Apostles taught, taking them from the lips of their Master. These are the same truths for which the confessors and the martyrs of all ages have given their life and their blood.

II
Mass of the Faithful

Gifts to the Most High

OFFERTORY

After the "Credo," the priest kisses the altar, then turns to the people and says:

℣. Dominus vobiscum. ℣. The Lord be with you.
℞. Et cum spiritu tuo. ℞. And with thy spirit.

With the words, "Oremus—Let us pray," he joins his hands and reads the "Offertory," inviting the faithful to follow the priest attentively and unite in the Sacrifice which he is about to commence.

In a broad sense, the *Offertory* includes all that part of the Mass from the *Creed* to the *Preface*. In a strict sense, it is applied only to the short antiphon which the celebrant recites immediately after the *Dominns vobiscum* following the *Creed*. It owes its name to the ancient practice observed by the faithful at this part of the Mass, of presenting their offerings of bread and wine at the altar to be consecrated at the Holy Sacrifice. The verse forming the *Offertory* is taken from Holy Scripture and, like the *Introit* and *Gradual*, is appropriate to the feast or season. The *Offertory of Corpus Christi* reads:

Sacerdotes Domini incensum et panes offerunt Deo: et ideo sancti erunt Deo suo, et non polluent nomen ejus. Alleluia.

The priests of the Lord offer incense and loaves to God, and therefore they shall be holy to their God, and shall not defile His Name. Alleluia!

United in the Lord, let us pray, not so much by words as by deeds and sentiments of the heart; not so much by begging and petitioning as by offering and self-surrender. For now the gift which is to be changed into the Body and Blood of Christ is prepared on the altar. Now is the acceptable time for each one to contribute his own offering so that afterwards he may have part in the Sacrifice of Christ. How can this be accomplished? In former times each person brought a visible gift to the altar—bread or wine, flowers, fruits, gold or other precious things—according to his means. With the visible gift he brought also an invisible one—the gift of readiness for sacrifice, which rendered his offering still more pleasing in the sight of God.

In our days, the faithful no longer offer bread and wine or like gifts, but the disposition of sacrifice is possible and necessary for each one of us. The present practice of making a collection or receiving the offerings of the faithful at this part of the Mass may be said to conform to the practice of early ages, as it is more convenient and suitable to the circumstances of our time for the people to make offerings of money instead of bread and wine, which offerings serve the same purpose—namely, the support of the priest, the supplying of the means requisite for the preservation and decoration of the altar and the church, and for the vestments and holy vessels required for the holy Sacrifice of the Mass. Then, too, we have gifts, spiritual gifts, which we can offer to the Lord. We should not neglect, in spirit, to place our offering on the paten to unite it with the offering of the priest. Have we, perhaps, a sorrow that weighs us down? Let it be our gift to the Lord, sanctified and made especially pleasing through the Cross of Christ. Let us offer our work and our good will; they are precious gifts. Has God perhaps lavished joys and prosperity upon us and blessed us abundantly? With a grateful heart let us offer them to Him. Every Christian is required to practice self-denial, to bear afflictions and privations. Let them be our gifts to the Most High. No one should come empty-handed, for God has given to each one something which he can and should now bring to Him as an offering.

St. Gertrude was accustomed to place herself upon the paten, in spirit, surrendering to God her body with all its senses and her soul with all its powers. Let us animate ourselves with the same sentiments, that, as St. Paul says, we may become a "living sacrifice, holy and pleasing to God."

The Spotless Host

With the "Offertory" the second part of Holy Mass is begun. The priest uncovers the chalice, places it at the side of the corporal, and presently with both hands raises the paten with the host and prays silently:—

Suscipe, sancte Pater, omnipotens aeterne Deus, hanc immaculatam hostiam, quam ego, indignus famulus tuus offero tibi Deo meo vivo et vero, pro innumerabilibus peccatis et offensionibus et negligentiis meis et pro omnibus circumstantibus, sed et pro omnibus fidelibus Christianis vivis atque defunctis, ut mihi et illis proficiat ad salutem in vitam aeternam. Amen.	Receive, O holy Father, Almighty Eternal God, this spotless host, which, I, thine unworthy servant, do offer unto Thee, my living and true God, for mine own countless sins, offenses, and negligences, and for all here present; as also for all faithful Christians, living or dead; that it may avail for my own and for their salvation unto life eternal. Amen.

> The priest raises his eyes to heaven when he elevates the host to denote that the oblation is made to God. Having finished the first words, he again lowers his eyes in token of his own unworthiness. After this prayer, he makes the Sign of the Cross with the paten in memory of the Sacrifice of the Cross about to be renewed. He then lays the host on the corporal.

BY THIS act of oblation, the priest presents the host as a sacrifice of atonement to the Most High. He calls it *spotless*, not because it was prepared with great care and of the finest flour, but because it is to become the true stainless gift, the Body of our Lord Jesus Christ, whose offering will avail us all unto salvation. He asks God, in virtue of the spotless host, to forgive, first, his own sins, offenses and negligences; then, those of all present in the church; and finally, those of all the faithful, whether still living in this world or suffering in the flames of purgatory. This prayer demonstrates the all-embracing charity which the Church wishes us to exercise in our prayers, especially at Holy Mass. Notice also that the priest here enumerates singly the three categories of sins by which the human heart is prone to offend God: 1. *peccatis*—sins of *commission*, evil thoughts, words and deeds; 2. *offensionibus*—sins of *scandal*, disedification given to others, etc., and 3. *negligentiis*—sins of *omission*, neglected duties, acts of zeal, charity, etc. Let us be mindful, then, of this threefold character of our sins, and say this prayer with heartfelt sentiments of contrition, without which we cannot hope to obtain the pardon which we ask of God.

Mingling of Water and Wine

> With hands joined, the priest walks to the Epistle corner of the altar, takes the chalice in his left hand and with the right wipes the inside with the purificator. He then pours wine and water into the chalice (having first blessed the water[6]) while reciting this prayer:—

---

[6] *In Masses for the departed, the above prayer is said, but the water is not blessed.*

Deus, qui humanae substantiae dignitatem mirabiliter condidisti, et mirabilius reformasti: da nobis per hujus aquae et vini mysterium, ejus divinitatis esse consortes, qui humanitatis nostrae fieri dignatus est particeps, Jesus Christus Filius tuus Dominus noster. Qui tecum vivit et regnat in unitate Spiritus sancti Deus: per omnia saecula saeculorum. Amen.

O God, who in creating human nature didst marvelously ennoble it, and hast still more marvelously renewed it; grant that by the mystery of this water and wine, we may be made partakers of His Divinity who vouchsafed to become partaker of our humanity, Jesus Christ, Thy Son, our Lord, who liveth and reigneth with Thee in the unity of the Holy Ghost, one God world without end. Amen.

WATER and wine are commingled, in imitation of the mixture of water and wine[7] which at the Last Supper Our Lord changed into His Precious Blood. Jesus thereby typified two things in a mysterious and symbolic manner; first, that His Divine and human natures are united in a wonderful union, the wine, as the more precious beverage signifying His Divine nature, and the water His human nature; secondly, that we, too, by the mystery of this union, are permitted to become partakers of His Divine nature, as the water typifies mankind in general. The wine used at Mass is not blessed because it represents Christ, the Eternal Son of the Father, and the source of all benefits, of all blessings. In every Holy Mass water and wine are mixed anew. In like manner should we, by taking part in the Holy Sacrifice, become united with God each time anew to participate in His Divine life. Rightly do we compare our gifts to the few drops of water; for what are we and all we can give in comparison with our High Priest, Jesus Christ, and His Sacrifice? He it is who accepts our gifts and prayers in His own infinite surrender to His Father; He it is who changes water into the wine of salvation and makes it precious in the sight of God.

---

[7] *This is in accordance with the teaching of St. Thomas, based on the authority of Councils and tradition.*

The Chalice of Salvation

Returning to the middle of the altar, the priest, with both hands, raises the chalice containing the water and wine, and says:—

Offerimus tibi, Domine, calicem salutaris, tuam deprecantes clementiam: ut in conspectu divinae majestatis tuae, pro nostra et totius mundi salute, cum odore suavitatis ascendat. Amen.	We offer unto Thee, O Lord, the chalice of salvation, beseeching Thy clemency that in the sight of Thy Divine Majesty it may ascend with the savor of sweetness, for our salvation and for that of the whole world. Amen.

IT IS called the "chalice of salvation" because the wine which it contains is to be changed into the Precious Blood which flowed for our eternal salvation. That this Sacrifice, the Sacrifice of Christ, ascends as a sweet odor, is told us by the Apostle: "Christ also loved us and delivered Himself up for us as an offering and a sacrifice to God to ascend in fragrant odor" (Ephes. 5: 2).

St. Gertrude, in spirit, placed her heart in the chalice at the Offertory and prayed that all the words spoken over the chalice might be spoken over her heart; and that as the water and wine were to be changed into the Precious Blood of Jesus Christ, so her heart might be changed from one cold and lukewarm into a heart glowing with ardent love for God.

After the foregoing prayer, the priest makes the Sign of the Cross with the chalice, places it on the center of the corporal and covers it with the pall. He then inclines moderately and prays silently:

In spiritu humilitatis, et in animo contrito suscipiamur a te, Domine: et sic fiat sacrificium nostrum in conspectu tuo hodie, ut placeat tibi, Domine Deus.	In an humble spirit, and a contrite heart, may we be received by Thee, O Lord; and may our Sacrifice be so offered up in Thy sight this day that it may be pleasing to Thee, O Lord God.

This prayer recalls the words of the Psalmist: "A sacrifice to God is an afflicted spirit: a contrite and humble heart, O

Gifts to the Most High

God, Thou wilt not despise" (Ps. 50: 19). Begging God that our oblation may be acceptable, that our hearts may be changed and that we may be made worthy to be offered to the Most High with Jesus Christ, we continue with the priest, to implore God to change the bread and wine into the Body and Blood of Our Lord by the power of the Holy Spirit.

The adorable Sacrifice of the Mass is the most sublime work of the Holy Spirit; therefore we invoke the Holy Spirit, by virtue of the Cross of Christ, to bless the sacrifice we have prepared: —

Veni sanctificator, omnipotens aeterne Deus, bene ✠ dic hoc sacrificium tuo sancto nomini praeparatum.

Come, O Sanctifier, Almighty Eternal God, and bless this Sacrifice prepared for Thy holy Name.

At these words, the priest looking up to God, raises his hands, folds them reverently, and makes the Sign of the Cross over the oblation.

Washing of the Hands

The priest, with hands joined, goes to the Epistle side of the altar. The server pours water over the tips of the thumb and forefinger of both hands, which are dried while the priest recites part of Psalm twenty-five:—

Lavabo inter innocentes manus meas: et circumdabo altare tuum, Domine.
Ut audiam vocem laudis: et enarrem universa mirabilia tua.

I will wash my hands among, the innocent: and will compass Thine altar, O Lord.
That I may hear the voice of Thy praise: and tell of all Thy wondrous works.

Domine, dilexi decorem domus tuae; et locum habitationis gloriae tuae.
Ne perdas cum impiis, Deus, animam meam: et cum viris sanguinum vitam meam.

O Lord, I have loved the beauty of Thy house: and the place where Thy glory dwelleth
Destroy, not my soul with the wicked, O God: nor my life with men of blood.

In quorum manibus iniquitates sunt: dextera eorum repleta est muneribus.	In whose hands are iniquities: their right hand is filled with gifts.
Ego autem in innocentia mea ingressus sum: redime me, et miserere mei.	But I have walked in innocence: redeem me, and have mercy on me.
Pes meus stetit in directo: in ecclesiis benedicam te, Domine.	My foot hath stood in the straight way: in the churches I will bless Thee, O Lord.
Gloria Patri,[9] et Filio, et Spiritui Sancto.	Glory be to the Father; and to the Son, and to the Holy Ghost.
Sicut erat in principio; et nunc et semper: et in saecula saeculorum. Amen.	As it was in the beginning, is now, and ever shall be, world without end. Amen.

THIS ceremony, is symbolic of the cleanliness and purity of soul and body with which we should appear before God. At the beginning of Holy Mass we recited the *Confiteor*. This was to purify ourselves, to make our heart clean by sincere contrition. The washing of the fingers signifies our petition that Our Lord may wash us yet more from our iniquities, and cleanse us from our sins, according to the words of the psalm.

The washing of the hands which follows the offering of gifts was customary even in ancient times. It is a symbol of purity. Formerly, not only the priest who sacrificed washed his hands, but also he who served at the altar. With pure hands, and also with pure hearts, should the Holy Sacrifice be offered. By the washing of the hands we are reminded of how Our Lord, by the washing of the feet of His disciples, prepared them for the reception of Holy Communion. The Church never forgets a single detail or lesson coming from that holiest of evenings, which means so much for us and for

---

[8] *In Masses for the departed and at Passiontide "Gloria Patri" is not said.*

our salvation. Accordingly, in every Mass there is a washing, not of the feet, but of the hands. It symbolizes the need of forgiveness of sins by repentance and prayer. Having voiced our repentance in the *Confiteor*, we now, in the *Lavabo*, pray for the complete forgiveness of sins which Christ alone can effect in our souls.

OBLATION TO THE HOLY TRINITY

Having finished the twenty-fifth psalm, the priest returns to the center of the altar, and bowing down, with hands joined, humbly entreats the Most Holy Trinity to receive the oblation which he is about to offer. He raises his eyes for a moment to the Crucifix enthroned on the altar; then, with bowed head, he makes the offering of his gifts to the Most Blessed Trinity, saying:

Suscipe, sancta Trinitas, hanc oblationem quam tibi offerimus ob memoriam passionis, resurrectionis et ascensionis Jesu Christi Domini nostri, et in honorem beatae Mariae semper Virginis, et beati Joannis Baptistae et sanctorum Apostolorum Petri et Pauli et istorum, et omnium Sanctorum; ut illis proficiat ad honorem nobis autem ad salutem; et illi pro nobis intercedere dignentur in coelis quorum memoriam agimus in terris. Per eumdem Christum Dominum nostrum. Amen.

Receive, O Holy Trinity, this offering which we make to Thee, in remembrance of the Passion, Resurrection and Ascension of our Lord Jesus Christ, and in honor of blessed Mary ever Virgin, of blessed John the Baptist, of the holy Apostles Peter and Paul, of these and of all the saints that it may avail to their honor and our salvation: and may they vouchsafe to intercede for us in heaven whose memory we celebrate on earth. Through the same Christ our Lord; Amen.

THE entire offering is summed up in this beautiful prayer. The priest turns to the Triune God and to the whole Church Triumphant. He places himself in communion with the heavenly court to invite them to participate in the adorable Sacrifice. In this prayer the priest begs the Holy Trinity to receive the offerings of bread and wine which are to be changed into Christ's Body and Blood, in honor of Christ's sufferings, Resurrection, and Ascension, in honor of the Blessed Virgin Mary and of all the saints. By thus honoring the saints we obtain their intercession and salvation through Jesus Christ.

Although there are many ways whereby we may honor Our Lady and afford her pleasure, none of the accidental joys we thus procure her equals that which we can give her by assisting at Holy Mass. For, since the glory of God and the salvation of sinners are what she loves and desires above all things, it affords her inexpressible joy to see us, by piously assisting at Holy Mass, offering to the Holy Trinity the worthiest service, praising, venerating, invoking, rejoicing the Most High, and presenting to Him the most precious of all gifts.

Every time Holy Mass is said, Jesus is born anew in a mystical manner, and the Blessed Virgin Mary's high dignity of Mother of God is renewed. Mary sees us, moreover, worshiping her beloved Son with steadfast faith, humbling ourselves before Him in lowly adoration. She sees us striking our breasts with penitent hearts and earnestly imploring the forgiveness of our sins. She looks with complacency on the offering we make to the Heavenly Father of the Body and Blood of her Divine Son for the cleansing and healing of our souls. Can we doubt, then, that she will favor us with her loving and powerful intercession in return for the joy and honor we offer her?

The best means of honoring the saints is likewise the offering of the holy Sacrifice of the Mass to God for their glory. Although the Mass is the renewal of Our Lord's Sacrifice on Calvary and is offered-up to Almighty God alone, the saints derive joy and glory from it, as St. Chrysostom testifies: "When a public ovation is offered to a king, the officers who have shared with him the perils of war and have borne themselves valiantly, are also mentioned by name, that they may likewise share in the glory of his triumph. So it is with the saints. They are honored and glorified in the presence of their Lord when His Passion and Death are triumphantly represented in Holy Mass. Then they, too, receive special mention, and the heroic deeds they achieved against their hellish foe are lauded and magnified. Then glory is given to Almighty God for the might wherewith He fortified them in the strife, and for the grace by means of which He secured to them the victory.

Another spiritual writer testifies: "One can give no greater satisfaction to the saints than by offering the Holy Mass to God in their name, thanking Him for the gifts He bestowed on them, commemorating their meritorious deeds, and offering these to the Holy Trinity in union with the Sacrifice of the Mass."

Orate, Fratres

The priest bends and kisses the altar as if to salute Jesus Christ after this prayer in which he has once more offered the Sacrifice to the Most Blessed Trinity. Next he turns to the faithful, extends and rejoins his hands, while he greets them with the words "Orate, fratres—Pray, brethren." Then, turning to the altar, he finishes the prayer silently:

Ut meum ac vestrum sacrificium acceptabile fiat apud Deum Patrem omnipotentem.

That my Sacrifice and yours may be acceptable to God the Father Almighty.

The server, on behalf of the faithful, responds:

Suscipiat Dominus sacrificium de manibus tuis, ad laudem et gloriam nominis sui, ad utilitatem quoque nostram, totiusque Ecclesiae; suae sanctae.

May the Lord receive the Sacrifice at thy hands, to the praise and glory of His Name, to our benefit, and to that of all His Holy Church.

℟. Amen.

℟. Amen.

AT various times during the Mass, the priest has said, *"Oremus* — Let us pray." This new invitation, *"Orate, fratres*—Pray, brethern," this new petition for the faithful to join with him in prayer, is to impress upon us that the nearer we approach to the moment of Consecration, the nearer we approach to Christ and the greater need we have of recollection and prayer.

Holy Mass—My Sacrifice

"MY Sacrifice and *yours*," says the priest. Yes, each one of us can truly say, "Holy Mass is *my* Sacrifice." "When you hear Mass," the learned Sanchez says, "remember that this Sacrifice is your possession, which is donated to you by God the Father and the Son." If we could realize this, Holy Mass would soon be considered by us the most holy, the most sublime and God-pleasing act of Divine worship.

To the devout Catholic, Holy Mass is not merely a form of prayer—it is an act of worship and a sacrifice; for, all who devoutly assist at Holy Mass offer the Divine oblation together with the priest. First of all, there is the great High Priest, the chief sacrificer, Jesus Christ, who Himself offers every Holy Mass to His Heavenly Father. Then there is the officiating priest, who immolates the Divine Victim. Thirdly, there are the faithful present at the Holy Sacrifice, who have the power of offering it in union with the priest.

One of the greatest graces granted to the children of the Church is that the privilege of offering to the Divine Majesty the sacred and sublime Sacrifice of the Mass is not the prerogative of priests alone, but, in a relative manner, belongs to the laity as well, to men, women, and children. Saint Peter lays stress on this prerogative when he says: "You, however, are a chosen race, a royal priesthood, a holy nation, a purchased people" (1 Peter 2: 9).

When we offer the Mass by the hands of the priest, we offer what is better than a spiritual oblation, namely, a visible one, even the self-same Victim whom the priest, holds in his hands. Happy indeed are we in being thus privileged, through the Divine bounty, to possess the inestimable treasure of the Body and Blood of Christ, and with a few words to offer It to God for our own immeasurable profit! This sacrificial act is the chief, the most important part, of hearing Mass, for without it we will neither gain much profit to ourselves nor give pleasure to God. It is not enough to be present at Mass in order to share in the fruits of the Mass; we must make a definite offering of it to God in union with the officiating priest.

The council of Trent teaches that by assisting at Holy Mass, the merits of our Lord Jesus Christ, the fruits of His Life, Passion and Death, are freely communicated to and bestowed upon us. Wherefore, since what we receive as a gift is as completely our own as what we earn ourselves, we are able at the time of Mass to present the merits of Jesus Christ to God the Father as our own oblation, and thereby give infinite satisfaction to His Divine Majesty. With what complacency must not the Heavenly Father regard us when we offer Him so precious a gift!

We can do nothing better during the time of Holy Mass than to make an act of oblation. The more frequently and fervently we do this, the more we please God, the more satisfaction we make for our sins and the more reward we lay up for ourselves in heaven. As often as we make this oblation to God, it is as if we said to Him: "I pay Thee this price for the remission of the temporal, punishment due to my sins, for the purchase of celestial treasures, for the relief of the suffering souls in purgatory."

It is indeed highly profitable for us to say at any time: "My God, I offer Thee Thy beloved Son; I offer Thee His Passion and Death; I offer Thee His virtues and His merits." But this act has a twofold value when it is uttered during the celebration of Holy Mass. At other times, this oblation is only one of the lips and of the heart; but during Holy Mass the oblation is a real and actual one, for then Our Lord Himself is really present in person and His merits are abundantly communicated to us; or rather, He gives Himself, that we may present Him to His Father. Oh, let us make frequent and fervent use of this glorious prerogative; it is the easiest way of acquiring eternal riches.

Let each one of us ever bear in mind: Holy Mass is *my* Sacrifice; it is *my* work; it is *my* possession. I unite myself with the priest, yes, with Jesus Christ Himself. Especially at the moment of Consecration should we bear in mind that we are not merely witnesses, but active participants in the offering of the Holy Sacrifice. Although the priest alone, as the representative of Christ, places the Divine Victim upon the altar by the words of consecration, and thus accomplishes the unbloody Sacrifice, we participate in the oblation in a limited sense, offering the Sacrifice by the hands of the priest and also to a certain extent, in union with him. Only the priest may take into his hands the Body of Our Lord and the Chalice with His Precious Blood; but we may do so in spirit, and unite with the priest in offering them to the Heavenly Father. This offering will be most pleasing to God, and will be still more acceptable to Him if we offer ourselves in union with Jesus.

Secret

AFTER calling upon the faithful to unite their prayers, with his that he may offer them collectively to the Heavenly Father, the priest prays, in silence and with outstretched hands, the special Offertory prayer called the *Secret*. This prayer should be said with deep interior sentiments. The faithful should be exceedingly attentive and exhibit the deepest respect, inasmuch as the priest is now entering into the holiest part of the Mass. The memorial of Christ's Passion is about to be celebrated, and the hearts of all present should be filled with awe and reverence.

The *Secret* is a prayer of petition, wherein we beseech God to deign graciously to accept the oblation, or we implore special gifts and graces needful for our earthly pilgrimage or for our eternal salvation. These graces we hope to obtain as fruits of the Sacrifice being offered. The *Secret* varies according to the feast or ecclesiastical season. Other *Secret* prayers may be added, corresponding to the Collects which have been prayed. The *Secret* of the Mass of Corpus Christi demonstrates the strength and beauty of these prayers:

Ecclesiae tuae, quaesumus Domine, unitatis et pacis, propitius dona concede: quae sub oblatis muneribus mystice designantur. Per Dominum...	In Thy mercy, O Lord, we beseech Thee, grant to Thy Church the gifts of unity and peace, which are mystically shown forth in the offerings we make to Thee. Through Our Lord...

Preface

Having finished the last prayers of the "Secret," the priest joins his hands as if to collect the hearts of all those present, to offer them to God as a sacrifice. He then disjoins his hands, places the right hand on the altar, and with the left turns the pages of the Missal. Thereupon he chants "the solemn prayer of praise and thanksgiving" which the early Christians in their language called "Eucharistia," that is, thanksgiving. He begins with a short preface (Prefatio) which has given the name "Preface" to the entire prayer. In the early centuries, there was a different Preface for most Masses. Later, the number was reduced to eleven, but a few special Prefaces have been introduced in recent years.

THE *Preface* is a beautiful hymn of praise and thanksgiving to God, which has been used from the earliest days of Christianity. With the words: "*Per omnia saecula saeculorum*—World without end," the priest closes the *Secret*. The server answers: *Amen*. We need God's special graces so that we may be able to join in the hymn of praise with love and devotion. The priest then secures for himself, as before every public prayer, the united support of those present: "*Dominus vobiscum* — The Lord be with you." "*Et cum spiritu tuo* — And with thy spirit," comes the answer. Raising his hands symbolically, he chants: "*Sursum corda!* —Lift up your hearts" We answer: "*Habemus ad Dominum*—We have them lifted up to the Lord."

"In this sublimest of hours," says the holy Bishop Cyril of Jerusalem, "our hearts should be turned heavenward to God and not downward to earth and our worldly affairs. It is as if the priest in this hour commanded us to forget all the cares of this life, all domestic griefs, and to raise our hearts to the good God in heaven.

"By our answer, we respond to his summons. Let none of us be so disposed as to say with our lips, 'We have them with the Lord,' and yet in spirit be occupied with the cares of this life."

> The priest joins his hands and proceeds: "Gratias agamus Domino Deo nostro— let us give thanks to the Lord our God!" to which the people respond: "Dignum et justum est—It is meet and just." Convinced that he is speaking in the name of the entire congregation, the priest turns to God, extends his hands and solemnly continues:

Vere dignum et justum est, aequum et salutare, nos tibi semper et ubique gratias agere, Domine sancte Pater omnipotens, aeterne Deus:[9] *quia per incarnati Verbi mysterium, nova mentis nostrae oculis lux tuae claritatis infulsit: ut dum visibiliter Deum cognoscimus, per hunc in invisibilium amorem rapiamur. Et ideo cum Angelis et Archangelis, cum Thronis et Dominationibus, cumque omni militia coelestis exercitus, hymnum gloriae tuae canimus, sine fine dicentes: Sanctus etc.*	It is truly meet and just, right and availing unto salvation, that we should at all times and in all places give thanks unto Thee, O holy Lord Father Almighty, everlasting God,[10] for by the mystery of the Word made Flesh the light of Thy glory hath shown anew upon the eyes of our mind; so that while we acknowledge Him as God seen by men, we may be drawn by Him to the love of things unseen. And therefore with the angels and the archangels, the thrones and dominions, and the whole host of the heavenly army, we sing the hymn of Thy glory, saying again and again: *Sanctus*, etc.

Thus the priest, with majestic words, praises the greatness of the Triune God and at the same time thanks Him for the revelation, of His glory. Let us take special, notice of the words: "*Semper et ubique*— always and everywhere." Should not the life of every man be a ceaseless song of praise and thanksgiving? A song of praise to God in the vicissitudes of life, which often bring joys but more often sorrows? A song of praise in sickness, on the deathbed? Everything comes from the hand of God. There is not a moment of our life which does not demand gratitude to God: *always and everywhere*. Ah, let us never forget! Praise and honor to God! What a glorious mission!

And as we are not able ourselves to send up worthy songs of praise and adoration to the throne of God, we have need of a Mediator, we have need of a Savior. Therefore, immediately

---

[9] *From this point the Preface changes, according to the feast or the liturgical season. The Preface of the Mass of Corpus Christi is that of Christmas, which emphasizes the close relation of the incarnation to the Holy Eucharist*

after having proclaimed that it is meet and just to praise God, the priest adds: *"Per Christum Dominum nostrum*—Through Christ our Lord."[10] In these few words the sublime meaning of Holy Mass is impressed upon us. We are told in what way our homage reaches God most surely. Our worship is rendered pleasing in the sight of the adorable Majesty through Jesus Christ, our Savior.

It is regrettable that great numbers of the faithful attach so little meaning to the liturgy of the Mass. How few, for example, consider the importance of the beautiful oft-repeated conclusion: "Through Christ our Lord." With God, however, these words have the same weighty significance as the signature of the sovereign ruler has with a minor civil authority.

"Through Christ our Lord" is the Divine seal impressed upon the humble petition of man. And immediately the poor, wretched human petition becomes a Divine mandate. This power lies within the Name of Jesus. If the endorsement of this Name is lacking to our supplication, our supplication is without worth.

Amid Angel Throngs

Sanctus and Benedictus

THE sublime words of the *Preface* still linger on our lips. We praise the Triune God, we give thanks for His goodness in Himself and for His benefits to us. But, realizing our unworthiness, we entreat God at the close of the *Preface* to permit us to join our feeble voices with the angels and archangels, with the cherubim and seraphim, who in all humility and reverence cease not to cry out with united voices:

---

[10] *The Preface for Corpus Christi, which is that of Christmas, is an exception.*

| Sanctus, sanctus, sanctus Dominus Deus Sabaoth. Pleni sunt coeli et terra gloria tua: Hosanna in excelsis. Benedictus qui venit in nomine Domini: Hosanna in excelsis. | Holy, holy, holy, Lord God of hosts. Heaven and earth are full of Thy glory. Hosanna in the highest. Blessed is He who cometh in the Name of the Lord. Hosanna in the highest. |

At the "Sanctus," the priest joins his hands and inclines moderately. The bell is rung thrice. At the words, "Benedictus qui venit," the priest stands erect and makes the Sign of the Cross on himself and at the words, "Hosanna in excelsis," he joins his hands again.

At the sound of the sanctuary bell, a solemn hush falls upon the assembled faithful. All kneel as the priest recites the *Sanctus*. This *Sanctus* is a joyous cry of praise to God. We, poor creatures, are permitted to sing the sacred *trisagion* which is unceasingly sung at the throne of God!

We read of the triumphant entry of Christ into Jerusalem that "the crowds that went before Him and those that followed kept crying out, saying, 'Hosanna to the Son of David! Blessed is He who comes in the Name of the Lord' " (Matt. 21: 9). "Hosanna in the highest" (Mark 11: 10). As Jesus was praised on His entry into Jerusalem, so was He heralded at

His entry into this world. The multitudes that preceded Him were the succession of patriarchs and the just of the Old Testament, marching before Him through forty centuries, carrying their triumphal palms and singing hosanna to the King of ages. And the multitudes that follow Him are the martyrs and the saints of the Church, the confessors and virgins of every clime and condition, following one another through twenty centuries to our own day, when we still repeat this hymn of praise.

Hosanna is a Hebrew word used in the Mass; also *sabaoth*, which means *armies, hosts, legions.* "Hosanna in the highest," means, "May our Hosanna be ratified in heaven." *Hosanna* is an exclamation of praise, meaning "Save now," "Give Thy salvation." This was the way the chosen people welcomed our Savior and it is the way we now welcome Him to our midst. Oh, the sublimity of this moment! Let us remember that we are about to witness the most stupendous wonder in heaven and on earth. Behold, the great Lord of heaven and earth is about to descend upon the altar. Myriad angels prostrate in profound adoration. Let our glad hearts cry out: "Welcome, Jesus! Blessed art Thou who comest in the Name of the Lord!"

Prayers before the "Great Wonder"

The Canon

After concluding the "Preface," the priest places his right hand on the altar and with the left turns to the "Canon." He then joins his hands before his breast, extends and elevates them slightly. He raises his eyes to the Crucifix and immediately lowers them, devoutly joining his hands. Then, with his hands on the edge of the altar, and inclining profoundly, he begins the Canon. During the Holy Sacrifice whenever one hand is used to turn the pages of the Missal, the other is placed flat on the altar— beside the corporal before the Consecration, on the corporal afterwards.

Prayers before the "Great Wonder"

HE *Canon* comprises the group of prayers from the *Sanctus* to the *Pater Noster*. The words of consecration are its precious kernel. *Canon* means *rule*. Holy Church uses this word to signify that the Canon is the unchangeable rule according to which the Sacrifice of the New Law is offered. It is, with the exception of a few additions, of apostolic origin. It is quite certain that St. Gregory the Great (died 604) was the last who made an addition to the Canon. What a consolation it should be for us to realize that today we recite the same fixed form of prayer that has been in use in the Church for more than thirteen centuries. The priest recites the prayers of the *Canon* in a low voice, for it is befitting that we celebrate in silence what is most holy and mysterious. Priest and people should now withdraw into the secret of their hearts, "close the doors" of their senses, with reverence kneel before the face of God and pray with their hearts rather than with their lips.

Because the sufferings of Christ are to be renewed in a mystical manner during the part of the Holy Mass now to follow, a picture of the Crucifixion is placed at the beginning of the *Canon* in every Missal, thereby more vividly to remind the celebrant of the Passion of Christ.

Prayer of Oblation for the Church
(Te igitur)

Bending low, the priest kisses the altar, and asks God through Jesus Christ, to accept our offerings. He then rises, rejoins his hands and makes the Sign of the Cross three times over the host and chalice to show that it is through the Redeemer that we obtain the blessing of the three Persons of the Holy Trinity. The remainder of the prayer is said with hands extended.

Te igitur, clementissime Pater, per Jesum Christum Filium tuum Dominum nostrum supplices rogamus ac petimus, uti accepta habeas, et benedicas, haec ✠ dona, haec ✠ munera, haec ✠ sancta sacrificia illibata: in primis qua; tibi offerimus pro Ecclesia tua sancta catholica: quam pacificare, custodire, adunare, et regere digneris toto orbe terrarum, una cum famulo tuo Papa nostro N., et Antistite nostro N., et omnibus orthodoxis, atque catholicae et apostolicae fidei cultoribus.

Wherefore, O most merciful Father, we humbly pray and beseech Thee, through Jesus Christ, Thy Son, Our Lord, that Thou wouldst vouchsafe to receive and bless these ✠ gifts, these presents, ✠ these ✠ holy and unspotted sacrifices, which in the first place we offer Thee for Thy holy Catholic Church, that it may please Thee to grant her peace; as also to protect, unite and govern her throughout the world, together with Thy servant N., our Pope; N., our bishop; as also all orthodox believers and professors of the Catholic and Apostolic Faith.

POPE Benedict XIV considered the three prayers beginning *Te igitur, Memento* and *Communicantes* as only one prayer, since there is only one conclusion for the three, namely, "through the same Christ our Lord." This prayer, *Te igitur,* follows naturally after the *Preface,* in which God is called "holy Lord, Almighty Father, Eternal God," and it is addressed to God the Father through His Son, Jesus Christ, our Lord. The words: "These gifts, these presents, these sacrifices," are not a mere repetition of the same thought. *Gifts* signifies the bread, and wine which we have received as gifts from God, and which are shortly to be changed into the Body and Blood of Christ. *Presents* signifies that we make an offering to God of His own gifts which He has granted to us for our use. Holy and unspotted *sacrifices* signifies that these gifts and presents have been already presented and sanctified in order to be used for the Holy Sacrifice.

The Sacrifice of Calvary mystically renewed.

After this petition to God follows a prayer for Holy Church, that God may pacify, protect, unify and govern her. Holy Church has many battles to fight and she needs this intercessory prayer during the adorable Sacrifice. She continues the mission of Christ upon earth, and must therefore be conformed to Him in all things. As He was subjected to sorrows and persecutions all during the course of His life of thirty-three years, so the history of the life of the Church down through the ages has been one of opposition and contradiction, of bloody persecution. The blood of martyrs, however, remains ever the seed of Christians, and with almost incredible fecundity Holy Church has increased and spread to the remotest corners of the earth. The prayers of her faithful children rise heavenward during the adorable Sacrifice, in union with the prayer of Christ, petitioning for her the Divine protection that she may ever stand serene and unharmed upon the Rock whereon her Founder placed her, unimpaired by the ravages of time and the wicked designs of men. Prayer and sacrifice made for the Church benefit the whole world. The more exalted she is, interiorly and exteriorly, the more abundant blessings she pours out upon humanity. The more gloriously she triumphs over her enemies, the more abundantly is fulfilled in her that promise of Jesus: "Behold I am with you all days even to the consummation of the world" (Matt. 28: 20).

After praying for the Church in general, a special petition is added for the Sovereign Pontiff and the diocesan bishop. Great responsibilities rest upon our ecclesiastical superiors; the welfare of mankind depends largely upon their fidelity to duty; therefore we implore the Divine assistance in their behalf. A third petition is added, for the faithful Catholics throughout the world.

WHERE REMEMBRANCE IS PRECIOUS
(Commemoration of the Living)

NO ONE can read the prayers of the Canon of the Mass attentively without realizing both the thoughtfulness of our holy Mother the Church, and the tremendous value of her remembrance. She gives us an example of her tender care by placing upon the lips of the priest and upon our lips a petition not only for the faithful in general, but for the individual persons for whom the Holy Mass is offered.

During the Memento for the Living, the priest slowly raises and joins his hands. While in this attitude of prayer, the names are pronounced of all those for whom he intends specially to pray. The priest then disjoins his hands, lowering them as before, and continues the Commemoration:

Memento, Domine, famulorum famularumque tuarum N. et N. et omnium circumstantium, quorum tibi fides cognita est, et nota devotio: pro quibus tibi offerimus, vel qui tibi offerunt hoc sacrificium laudis, pro se, suisque omnibus, pro redemptione animarum suarum, pro spe salutis et incolumitatis suae; tibique reddunt vota sua aeterno Deo, vivo et vero.	Be mindful, O Lord, of Thy servants and handmaids, N. and N. and of all here present, whose faith and devotion are known to Thee: for whom we offer, or who offer up to Thee this Sacrifice of praise, for the redemption of their souls, for the hope of their safety and salvation, and who now pay their vows to Thee the eternal, living and true God

In the first prayer of the *Canon*, the priest prays for those for whom the Holy Sacrifice is especially offered; as, for example, the parishioners, those who have given the stipend and requested the Mass to be said for their intention; those for whom the priest wishes expressly to pray, as, for example, his parents and relatives; those who have recommended themselves to his prayers; and, finally, all those present.

Devout persons have at all times considered this *Memento* at Holy Mass of great value. And how touching is the thought that in this Memento the priest has the power to bring to God intentions and petitions, cares and sorrows, from souls who perhaps have sought help and consolation everywhere else in vain, for whom no other hand or voice is raised but that of the priest at the altar. Who knows how many hopes are again revived by these few minutes at the altar: so many crosses and intentions have been confided to the priest; — sufferings of which he alone knows. For these and for all he sends up his prayer to heaven, reanimated by the hope that

God will condescend graciously to grant these petitions in virtue of the Holy Sacrifice.

"Fellow-citizens with the Saints"
(Communicantes)

HAVING remembered the manifold needs of the Church Militant through the "Commemoration of the living," we now raise our eyes to the Church Triumphant with which we are united through the Communion of Saints:—

Communicantes, et memoriam venerantes, in primis gloriosae semper Virginis Mariae, genitricis Dei et Domini nostri Jesu Christi: sed et beatorum Apostolorum ac Martyrum tuorum, Petri et Pauli, Andreae, Jacobi, Joannis, Thomas, Jacobi, Philippi, Bartholomasi, Matthaei, Simonis et Thaddaei: Lini, Clett, Clementis, Xysti, Cornelii, Cypriani, Laurentii, Chrysogoni Joannis et Pauli, Cosmae et Damiani, et omnium sanctorum tuorum; quorum meritis precibusque concedas, ut in omnibus protectionis tuae muniamur auxilio. Per eumdem Christum Dominum nostrum. Amen.	In communion with, and honoring the memory, first of the glorious, ever Virgin Mary, Mother of our God and Lord Jesus Christ; as also of Thy blessed Apostles and Martyrs, Peter and Paul, Andrew, James, John Thomas, James, Philip, Bartholomew, Matthew, Simon, and Thaddeus Linus, Cletus, Clement, Xystus, Cornelius, Cyprian, Lawrence, Chrysogonus John and Paul, Cosmas and Damian and of all Thy saints; by whose merits and prayers grant that we may in all things be defended by the aid of Thy protection. Through the same Christ our Lord. Amen.

On a number of the high festivals of the year, mention of the mystery commemorated is interwoven in this prayer.

The fact that in this commemoration mention is made only of the Apostles and martyrs and not of confessors indicates that the Canon was introduced prior to the fourth century when only the former, and not the latter, were honored as saints.

Prayers before the "Great Wonder"

The prayers of the holy Catholic Church and the faithful are strengthened by the intercession of the holy Mother of God and all the elect. The priest turns first to the Blessed Virgin Mary, for she brought forth our Divine Savior, who will soon be present under the appearances of bread and wine. She is above all saints and angels because of her merits, her graces, her prerogatives and her exalted glory in heaven as the Mother of the only-begotten Son of God. She was beside our Savior at His bloody Sacrifice on the Cross; she offered herself with Him for us; hence her name is inseparable from the Holy Sacrifice.

At the name "Maria" the priest inclines his head toward the Missal, and at "Jesu Christi," toward the Crucifix.

The priest then mentions by name the eleven faithful Apostles who were with Our Lord at the Last Supper, the pillars of the Church, the fathers of our Faith, and as a twelfth adds the holy Apostle Paul, whose name is always associated with that of St. Peter in the liturgy of the Church. To the Apostles are united twelve of the most illustrious martyrs who watered the foundation of the Church with their blood. Linus, Cletus and Clement were fellow-laborers with St. Peter in preaching the Gospel in Rome, and all three severally became his successors in the pontifical chair. Xystus and Cornelius also were popes; the former was martyred about A.D. 129; the latter in the year 252. Cyprian was the celebrated bishop and martyr of Carthage. Lawrence (✠ Aug. 10, 258) was deacon to Pope Xystus II. Chrysogonus was an illustrious Roman, martyred at Aquileia under Diocletian and buried in Rome. John and Paul were brothers who, rather than worship marble gods and idols, underwent a cruel death by order of Emperor Julian the Apostate. Cosmas and Damian, also martyred under Diocletian, were physicians who for the love of God and their neighbor exercised their profession gratis.

Oh wonderful spiritual union between the saints in heaven and the faithful on earth! Millions of Catholic Christians daily present their petitions before the throne of the Godhead, crying: "Have mercy on us." But the consciousness of their guilt gives just reason to fear that these petitions will not always be granted. Therefore they turn with confidence to those beloved friends of God who have already gained the crown of victory, and plead with them to intercede in their behalf. And the hosts of saints lovingly approach the throne of Divine Mercy, and, pointing to their beloved brethren still combating on the battlefield of earth, pray: "Lord, for the sake of the love Thou hearest us, have mercy on them." Thus, through the merits and intercession of the saints, many graces are obtained which would not otherwise have been granted.

The glorious choir of Apostles and Martyrs whom we invoke with the Blessed Virgin Mary were once wayfarers on this earth, but now joyously wave their palms before the throne of the King of martyrs, the Divine Lamb. They know our needs and are interested in our welfare. As children of the same family, we form with them the communion of the kingdom of Jesus Christ. Owing to God's goodness, there exists between them and us a constant intercourse, a mutual giving and receiving. Prayer, good works and sufferings, — in fact, all fruits of grace, are common possessions, from which every one draws and to which every one contributes his share. During the adorable Sacrifice, as we draw closer to the Most High, we realize our unworthiness, and we then appreciate more fully what a great blessing it is to belong to such a glorious communion—to be "citizens with the saints and members of God's household" (Ephes. 2: 19).

A FOURFOLD PETITION
(HANC IGITUR)

The second prayer of the "Canon" is now recited. When beginning the "Hanc igitur," the priest spreads his hands over the oblation so that the tips of his fingers reach as far as the middle of the pall. The bell is then rung once, to announce the coming of Christ on the altar.

Hanc igitur oblationem servitutis nostrae sed et cunctae familiae tuae, quaesumus Domine, ut placatus accipias, diesque nostros in tua pace disponas, atque ab aeterna damnatione nos eripi, et in electorum tuorum jubeas grege numerari. Per Christum Dominum nostrum. Amen.

We therefore beseech Thee, O Lord, graciously to accept this oblation of our service, as also of Thy whole family; dispose our days in Thy peace, command us to be delivered from eternal damnation and to be numbered in the flock of Thy elect. Through Christ our Lord. Amen.

THE first petition contained in this prayer is that God may accept the oblation of our service. As creatures, our first duty to our Creator is the service of adoration, praise, thanksgiving and homage. This service, through the infinite mercy of God, we are capable of fulfilling adequately through Jesus Christ our Lord, who, on the Calvary of the altar, as on the altar of Calvary, is the most complete sacrifice of adoration, the most sublime sacrifice of praise, the noblest sacrifice of thanksgiving and the truest oblation of our homage.

The second petition is that God may dispose our days in peace. Daily, if not hourly, there are battles to be fought; there are vices to be checked, the world and its seductions to be conquered, the cunning snares of hell to be vanquished, the attacks of Satan to be repulsed.

The third petition is that we may be delivered from eternal damnation. It is very significant that in the solemn moment immediately preceding the descent of the Son of God upon the altar. Holy Church reminds us of the danger of eternal perdition. Never can we pray sufficiently for God to preserve us from it. This grace we must obtain at all costs; otherwise our suffering's here below would be but the beginning of a painful despair in eternity where there is no hope.

Finally, we knock at the door of God's mercy, begging Him to grant us life everlasting and to count us among the number of His elect. Our great aim in life is to serve God and to attain heaven, where, in joy, love, bliss and happiness, we shall forever reign with the Triune God and the blessed.

The recitation of this prayer is accompanied by a very beautiful ceremony. As mentioned above, the priest stretches forth his hands over the offering and begs God graciously to accept it. It was a common ceremony in the Old Law for the priest to hold his hands extended over the victim which was about to be offered up in sacrifice. By this ceremony was expressed the act of consecrating the animal as a victim praying that God would transfer the iniquities of His people to the head of the victim and accept its immolation in place of the death which they deserved for their sins. In the same manner we confidently ask the Almighty Father to look down upon His only Son who is to appear on the altar in the state of an expiring victim, and for His sake and for His sufferings to divert our sins from us.

Bloody and Unbloody Sacrifice Identified by the Cross
(Quam Oblationem)

At the conclusion of the "Hanc Igitur" the priest rejoins his hands, and draws them towards himself, saying the third prayer of the "Canon":

PRAYERS BEFORE THE "GREAT WONDER"

Quam oblationem tu, Deus, in omnibus, quaesumus, bene ✠ dictam, adscrip ✠ tam, rationabilem, acceptabilemque facere digneris: ut nobis Cor ✠ pus et San ✠ guis fiat dilectissimi Filii tui Domini nostri Jesu Christi.	Which oblation do Thou, O God, vouchsafe in all things to make blessed, ✠ approved, ✠ ratified, ✠ reasonable, and acceptable, that it may become for us the Body ✠ and ✠ Blood of Thy most beloved Son, our Lord Jesus Christ.

Host and chalice are now repeatedly signed with the Sign of the Cross, not only before the Consecration, but also after. While saying the "Quam oblationem" the priest blesses the oblation, three crosses being made over the host and chalice, followed by one cross over the host and another above the chalice. He then joins his hands and inclines his head to the Crucifix at the sacred Name with which the blessing ends.

IN GENERAL, the oft-repeated Sign of the Cross is not only symbolic; a blessing is also imparted with it. The gifts, as well as the hearts of those who offer them, should by this Sign of the Cross be cleansed and sanctified before the Consecration. After the Consecration, the hearts of the priest and the faithful are blessed by this sacred sign for the actual or spiritual Communion, for the intimate union with Christ.

Not only in a general way should the identity that exists between the bloody and the unbloody Sacrifice of Christ be made clear to us by the Sign of the Cross; we can piously and edifyingly consider the five repetitions of the Sign of the Cross, in this prayer occurring immediately before, and in another prayer, directly after the Elevation, as indicating the five Sacred Wounds which were most prominent on the Body of Christ, and which, consequently, are also in the most intimate relation with the redeeming Passion and Death of Our Lord. At the same moment in which the altar, by the presence of the Divine Victim, becomes a mystical Mount Calvary, the sublime and sacred scene of the Passion of our Savior, crucified and covered with painful wounds, may well present itself before the eyes of the priests and people.

With this prayer, the preparation for the Consecration is completed. For the last time the priest entreats God to raise to their supreme perfection the gifts dedicated to Him by changing them into the Body and Blood of Christ.

The Heart of the Mass

Consecration and Elevation

Three parts of the Mass were instituted by our Savior, namely, the *Offertory*, the *Consecration* and the *Communion*. "The *Offertory*," says Father von Cochem, "is the giving of thanks and blessing of the bread and wine, whereby both are dedicated to the service of God. This was done at the Last Supper when Our Lord took bread and wine, gave thanks to His Heavenly Father, and blessed them.

"The *Consecration* consists in the *repetition* of the words which Christ spoke on that memorable occasion: 'This is My Body... This is My Blood' (Matt. 26: 26,28). The *Consecration* is the most important part of the Mass, because by it Christ becomes present on our altars, and in it lies the essence of the sacrifice..."

"The *Communion* is the *consumption* of the sacred oblation. This was also done at the Last Supper when Our Lord gave His Flesh and Blood to be received by the Apostles under the forms of bread and wine." Full of faith and confidence, Holy Church now begs for the same sublime wonder as that which Our Lord performed at the Last Supper. What Our Lord did on that occasion, the priest now does in His stead. He takes the bread in both his hands, raises his eyes toward heaven, bows his head, blesses and speaks the holy words of Consecration: —

Qui pridie quam pateretur, accepit panem in sanctas ac venerabiles manus suas, et elevatis oculis in coelum, ad te, Deum, Patrem suum omnipotentem, tibi gratias agens, bene ✠ *dixit, fregit, deditque discipulis suis, dicens Accipite, et manducate ex hoc omnes. HOC EST ENIM CORPUS MEUM.*	Who, the day before He suffered, took bread into His holy and venerable hands, and with His eyes lifted up to heaven, unto Thee, God, His almighty Father, giving thanks to Thee, He blessed, ✠ broke and gave to His disciples, saying: Take and eat ye all of this, for THIS IS MY BODY.

At the words "Qui pridie," the priest wipes the tips of his thumbs and forefingers lightly on the corporal. Then he takes the host "between those fingers, and holding it thus with his hands raised a little above the corporal, he elevates his eyes to heaven at the words "elevatis oculis in coelum—with His eyes lifted up to heaven," and lowers them at once; and at the words "tibi gratias agens—giving thanks to Thee," he bows his head. At the word "Benedixit—He blessed," holding the host in his left hand, he makes the Sign of the Cross over it with his right hand, and continues the prayer "fregit deditque discipulis suis—broke and gave to His disciples," again taking the host with both hands, as before, and finishes the words "Accipite, et manducate ex hoc omnes —Take and eat ye all of this."

Having said these words, he rests his forearms upon the altar and inclines his head; holding the host in the manner just described, with the other fingers of both hands joined together, he pronounces the words of consecration over the large host and any small ones that may be on the corporal, "Hoc est enim Corpus Meum — for this is My Body." It is required that these words be said distinctly, reverently and secretly.

After the words of consecration, the priest removes his forearms from the altar, and, holding the Host with his thumbs and forefingers as before, genuflects slowly on one knee to the floor, without inclining his head, and with his eyes fixed on the Host; then, standing erect, he elevates the Host over the corporal, above his head, so that It may be seen by the people, always keeping his eyes fixed upon It. He thus elevates the Host that the people may adore It reverently and solemnly. Then he lowers It gently toward the corporal. When near the corporal, he places the Host upon it with the right hand alone, and again genuflects in adoration.

If there be a ciborium containing small Hosts, he replaces the cover after the second genuflection. From this moment until the last ablution the priest keeps the thumb and forefinger of each hand joined together, except when it becomes necessary to touch the Host.

"My Lord and My God!"

WHEN the Sacred Host is elevated, the faithful should look at It, if possible, and then bow their heads in adoration. Keeping the head bowed low during the Elevation at Mass is customary among many Catholics. Many are scrupulously conscientious not to look at the Sacred Host or the Chalice, lest thereby they might fail in reverence towards God. This practice originates in a good will, no doubt, but it is, nevertheless, not praiseworthy. People are under the impression that it is wrong to gaze at our Eucharistic God! O unhappy remnant of the age of Jansenism!

Holy Church holds an entirely different view; she desires that we devoutly *look* at the Blessed Sacrament. Otherwise, what significance would there

The greatest treasure we possess on earth and the hope of our reward is heaven is centered in the tiny consecrated Host.

be in the precept of the Church which obliges priests to elevate the Sacred Host, after the Consecration, high enough to be seen by the faithful? In fact, it was in protest of a false teaching about the Blessed Eucharist that the Church, in 1197,[11] ordered as a renewed act of faith and at the same time as an act of reparation, that the Sacred Host be elevated immediately after the Consecration. There have been, at times, controversies regarding the rubric of looking at the Sacred Host and Chalice at the moment of elevation. Some pointed out the direction in the Roman Missal that the priest show the consecrated Host and Chalice to the people, and drew the conclusion that therefore the people were intended also to look at them, supporting this conclusion by historical references. Others objected to this practice on various grounds — either that custom was against it, or that it seemed irreverent, etc. But on May 18, 1907, the Sacred Congregation of Indulgences put an end to all controversy by granting an indulgence to all the faithful who gaze at the Sacred Host with faith, devotion and love, either at the Elevation of the Mass or when It is solemnly exposed in the monstrance, saying at the same time: "My Lord and my God"[12] showing plainly by this action what the desires of Holy Church are with regard to the conduct of the faithful.

---

[11] *This false teaching was begun by Berengarius nearly two centuries previously, and the evil work was carried on after him by Tanchelm and later by Peter the Chanter.*

[12] *An indulgence of 7 years is granted, each time, to all the faithful who, at the Elevation of the Mass, or at public exposition of the Blessed Sacrament, devoutly say these words. (According to a more recent legislation, it is no longer required that one look at the Sacred Host.) This indulgence was extended to include the blind also, by Pope Pius X, May 9, 1912. If said daily, a plenary indulgence may be gained once a week after confession and Communion and prayers for the Pope's intention. ("Manual of Indulgences" 133)*

At the request of the Archbishop of Albi, France, Pope Benedict XV, in 1919, extended the indulgence granted by Pius X, during Mass at the moment of Elevation, to **the Benediction** *of the* **Most Blessed Sacrament.** *It may be gained by repeating those words while the celebrant makes the Sign of the Cross with the ostensorium.*

At the Elevation, the priest might in all justice say to the people: "Behold, O Christians, here is your Savior, your Redeemer, your Sanctifier. Contemplate Him with sincere faith; pour out your hearts to Him. 'Blessed are the eyes that see what you see' (Luke 10: 23)." Blessed, indeed, are the eyes that gaze with reverence on the Sacred Host and believe that Jesus is hidden under this lowly form. Each one of us can then say with the patriarch Jacob, "I have seen God face to face, and my soul has been saved." (Gen. 32: 30). And indeed we have a better right to employ these words than Jacob had, for he saw only an angel sent from God, whilst we gaze upon the Savior Himself, concealed under the appearance of bread.

How pleasing to God is the desire to gaze at Him, even though He is veiled by the Eucharistic species, can be judged from a revelation to St. Gertrude. This saint received from Our Lord the assurance that for every look of love and devotion which we turn to the Sacred Host, we merit an increase of glory in heaven; and when once we behold God face to face, we shall participate in as many special joys as we shall have directed, loving glances toward the Blessed Sacrament, or even desired to do so when prevented. What a glorious promise!

Is not this gazing upon the Eucharistic Savior a magnificent profession of our faith, in the real presence of Christ, as it was professed by the incredulous Apostle Thomas? When Thomas said, *My Lord and my God*, we may be sure he did not keep his eyes cast down, but looked with open and sincere gaze into the eyes of his Master. We do not, indeed, see Him with our bodily eyes as Thomas saw Him, but the light of faith clearly reveals to us that the Sacred Host at which we gaze is no longer earthly bread, but Jesus, the God-man, the immortal King of heaven and earth, who at the word of the priest has become present upon the altar. We believe that just as once at the angel's "Ave" He assumed human nature in the bosom of the Virgin Mary by the power of the Holy Ghost, so now by the sacred words of consecration, as man He becomes sacramentally present by the power of the same Holy Spirit.

Jesus, Our Mediator

HOW glorious a gift, how excellent an oblation, does the priest present to the Most Holy Trinity when he elevates the Sacred Host! But it is not the priest alone who performs this act. Jesus, our Divine Savior, places Himself before the eyes of God the Father and offers Himself to Him in so sublime a manner that no created intelligence is capable of comprehending it. We read in the revelations of St. Gertrude that she was privileged to see, during the Elevation of the Sacred Host, Our Lord with His own hands lifting on high His Heart in the form of a golden chalice, presenting Himself to the Heavenly Father and making the oblation of Himself for the faithful in a manner past human comprehension. And Our Lord revealed to St. Mechtilde: "I alone know, and perfectly understand, what this offering is that I daily make of Myself for the salvation of the faithful; it surpasses the comprehension of cherubim and seraphim, and all the hosts of heaven."

In the life of St. Colette, it is related that once when she was assisting at the Mass said by her confessor, she was heard at the Consecration, to exclaim: "O my God, my Jesus! O angels and saints, O men and sinners, what marvels are these that we see and hear!" After Mass her confessor asked what had made her cry out in this manner. She replied: "When your reverence elevated the Sacred Host, I beheld Christ upon the Cross, the Blood flowing from His precious Wounds; at the same time I heard Him thus address the Eternal Father:

Look upon My Wounds, look upon the Blood that I shed, consider My sufferings, consider My Death. All this I endured to save sinners. Now, if Thou dost consign them to perdition on account of their iniquities and deliver them over to the devil, what compensation shall I have for My bitter Passion, for My cruel Death? The reprobate sinners will render Me no thanks; on the contrary, they will curse Me for all eternity. But if they were saved they would praise and magnify Me forever in gratitude for My sufferings. For My sake, therefore, spare these sinners, O My Father, and preserve them from eternal damnation."

It is of greatest benefit to us to unite our prayer with that which our Divine Mediator offers for us upon the altar, imploring Him to make it one with His; for this union will render it so powerful that no other prayers can compare with it. In virtue of the merits of Christ's Passion, the prayers offered in union with the Holy Sacrifice have infinitely more value than any other prayers, however long or however fervent. Therefore, if we unite our poor petitions which we offer during Mass to the perfect prayer of Our Lord, they will, like a copper coin immersed in molten gold, be beautified and ennobled, and rendered meet to be borne to heaven as a precious oblation.

After the act of faith and the adoration of the Sacred Host, the act of oblation should follow. The oblation of the Body and Blood of Christ is the most real and powerful atonement for the guilt of man. In other words, there is no more efficacious means of appeasing the anger of God than offering to Him the Body and Blood of His Son there present on the altar. It is a very salutary practice, therefore, for all who are present at Mass to make this offering with all their heart for the remission of their sins. The following prayer may be used: "O Eternal Father, I offer Thee Thy beloved Son Jesus in the

Sacred Host, with all His love, all His sufferings, all His merits and all His perfections, to Thine everlasting praise and glory, in expiation for my sins and for the sins of the whole world."

"Hail, Precious Blood!"

AFTER this oblation follows the consecration of the wine and the elevation of the chalice, which has a special meaning and supernatural power, for by it the Precious Blood of Christ is shed in a mystical manner and sprinkled upon all those who are present. This is signified in the words of consecration:

Simili modo postquam coenatum est, accipiens et hunc praeclarum Calicem in sanctas ac venerabiles manus suas, item tibi gratias agens, bene ✠ *dixit, deditque discipulis suis, dicens: ACCIPITE, ET BIBITE EX EO OMNES: HIC EST ENIM CALIX SANGUINIS MEI, novi et aeterni testamenti; mysterium fidei: qui pro vobis et pro multis effundetur in remissionem peccatorum.*

In like manner, after He had supped, taking also this excellent Chalice into His holy and venerable hands, also giving thanks to Thee, He blessed ✠ and gave it to His disciples saying: TAKE AND DRINK YE ALL OF THIS. FOR THIS IS THE CHALICE OF MY BLOOD of the new and eternal testament; the mystery of faith, which shall be shed for you and for many for the remission of sins.

The celebrant, having adored the Sacred Host, places his left hand on the foot of the chalice and uncovers it with his right hand, placing the pall either on the veil or against the altar card. Then he purifies his fingers over the chalice, which he always does after touching the Host, lest any small particle should adhere to them. Whilst doing this, standing erect, he says: "Sumili modo postquam coenatum est—In like manner, after He had supped;" and, continuing, when uttering the words, "accipiens et hunc praeclarum calicem, etc.—taking also this excellent chalice," etc., he takes the chalice with both hands just under the cup, raises it a little, and replaces it immediately, saying the words, "item tibi gratias agens—also giving thanks to Thee," at which he inclines his head, not to the Crucifix, but to the Blessed Sacrament. At the word "benedixit—He blessed," he keeps his left hand holding the chalice in the same position under the cup, while he makes the Sign of the Cross over it with his right hand and continues with the words, "deditque discipulis suis,...— gave it to His disciples,..." Then, with both hands he holds the chalice raised a little, placing the three fingers of the left hand under the foot of the chalice to support it, and with head inclined, he pronounces attentively, reverently and secretly the words of Consecration: "Hic est enim Calix Sanguinis Mei novi et aeterni testamenti; mysterium fidei qui pro vobis et pro multis effundetur in remissionem peccatorum — For this is the Chalice of My Blood of the new and eternal testament; the mystery of faith: which shall be shed for you and for many, for the remission of sins."

After pronouncing the words of consecration, the celebrant places the Chalice on the corporal, genuflects slowly, saying at the same time the words:

Haec quotiescumque feceritis, in mei memoriam facietis.

As often as ye shall do these things, ye shall do them in memory of Me.

Then he takes the Chalice with the right hand, and supporting it by the three fingers of the left, he elevates is so that it may be seen by the people, keeping his eyes steadily fixed upon it. Without any delay, but with slow movement, he lowers the Chalice, places it in its usual place on the corporal and covers it with the pall, after which he genuflects once more in adoration of the Precious Blood of Christ now contained under the appearance of wine.

The acolyte raises the chasuble of the celebrant with his left hand at the elevation of the Host and of the Chalice, and with his right hand rings the bell three times at each elevation.

Our first sentiments after the Elevation should be those of worship, adoration, love, and thanksgiving. Jesus is present on the altar—Jesus, our loving Savior, who makes Himself our Sacrifice of adoration, thanksgiving, atonement and petition. As we exclaimed, with adoring love: "My Lord and my God!" at the moment of the elevation of the Sacred Host, so now we should adore the Precious Blood elevated in the chalice. The following aspiration is appropriate: "Hail, Precious Blood, flowing from the Wounds of Jesus and washing away the sins of the world! Oh, cleanse, sanctify and keep my soul, that nothing may ever separate me from Thee; in life and in death let me be Thine." Or the indulgenced prayer: "Eternal Father, I offer Thee the Precious Blood of Jesus Christ, in satisfaction for my sins, in supplication for the holy souls in purgatory and for the needs of Holy Church." (Ind. of 500 days each time. "Manual of Indulgences," 219.)

The oblation of the Precious Blood is most efficacious in turning away the Divine anger provoked by the transgressions of mankind, as was revealed to St. Mary Magdalen de Pazzi. At no time can this oblation be made so opportunely, so effectively, as after the Consecration in Holy Mass. It is then offered not only in word, but in very deed, for the Sacred Blood is truly and actually there in the chalice, and the offering is of far greater merit than at any other time. One single drop of this Precious Blood is worth more than oceans of the blood of martyrs. According to St. Thomas Aquinas, one single drop would have sufficed to redeem the whole world. There is no sin so heinous that it cannot be forgiven, no stain so dark that it cannot be purged away, no debt so enormous that it cannot be remitted through the power of the Precious Blood. Let us, therefore, unite with the priest and offer It to God after the Consecration with all our fervor.

During Holy Mass, let us also beseech the Blessed Virgin to offer to the Eternal Father the Blood of her Son in the chalice, for the whole Church, for the conversion of sinners, for the souls in purgatory, and for our various needs. We may be assured that we shall receive very special graces by this practice.

The Consecration is the heart of the Canon and of the entire Mass; yes, it is the fountain of the life of the Church.

For, as the blood flows from the heart to all parts of the body, so the Blood of the Redeemer, which was shed on the Cross, by the Consecration flows to all parts of the Catholic Church. The fivefold Cross with which the gifts are blessed at the beginning of the Consecration signifies the five Wounds by which Our Lord consummated His Sacrifice on the Cross.

Souls Sprinkled with the Precious Blood

IN HIS Passion the Blood of Christ was shed, but It fell upon the stones and the ground. In Holy Mass the selfsame blood is shed; but It does not fall upon the earth nor upon the bodies of men; It is applied to the souls of those who are present. Thus, when we assist at Holy Mass it is just as if we stood, beneath the Cross on Calvary, with contrition of heart, and were sprinkled with the Precious Blood. And as we should then have been cleansed from all stain of sin, so no less surely will we now be sprinkled with that same Blood, and, if we are repentant, be cleansed from guilt.

How unspeakable is the love of Jesus for us poor sinners! Is it really possible that our adorable Savior, who shed His Blood to the last drop for us on Calvary, should shed It again and again for us, daily, hourly, for the remission of our sins and for our eternal salvation? Great, indeed, are the graces, the blessings they receive who assist devoutly at Holy Mass!

Oh, how precious is the Victim on our altars! We can appropriate to ourselves His infinite merits by our good intention, by our contrition and love, by Holy Communion, but above all and beyond all, by fervently hearing Mass. These are the declarations of learned theologians, who tell us that by no means can we participate in the merits of Christ so surely as by assisting at Mass.

Just as Moses sprinkled the Jews with the blood of the sacrificial victims, and the priest sprinkles Christian people with holy water, so Christ spiritually sprinkles the souls of the faithful with His Blood which is shed for them in the Mass. St. Mary Magdalen de Pazzi says of this spiritual sprinkling: "This Blood, when applied to the soul, imparts to it as much dignity as if it were decked in a costly robe. It imparts such brilliance and splendor that, couldst thou behold the effulgence of thy soul when sprinkled with that Blood, thou wouldst fall down to adore it."

Happy the soul adorned with such beauty! Let us go to Holy Mass often, that we may be sprinkled with this adorable Blood and our soul arrayed in rich apparel which will render us glorious forever in the sight of the angels and saints. The Catholic Church owns no greater, no more costly treasure than the Precious Blood of Jesus Christ; for a single drop of this Blood, which is united to the Second Person of the Blessed Trinity, outweighs in value all the riches of heaven and of earth.

Mystical Death of Christ

THE "Great Wonder" has taken place. Christ, the true High Priest, has consummated the one true Sacrifice of the New Law which He offered for us on the Cross and which He causes to continue to be effective among us till the end of time. He indeed died but once and now dies no more, and yet He mysteriously represents to us His Death in a true and wonderful, although unbloody and mystical manner. The two separate forms visibly signify this mystery. Under each form Christ is indeed wholly and entirely present; for Our Lord changed not only bread, but also wine, and commanded His priests to do so also, because wine in a special manner signifies His Blood as It was shed and separated from His Body at His Death on the Cross. The forms in their separation are the symbol and sign of death. Under their cover, however, Christ is with us as He comes down to us from eternity—as the Glorified One, as the Conqueror, as the One risen from the dead, as our glorious Easter Lamb, which is, as it were, slain, and yet lives forever.

To excite our devotion, let us occupy our minds with the real, though concealed, presence of Jesus, now enthroned upon the altar, around which cherubim and seraphim are kneeling in lowly adoration. Nor should we forget that this is really the Sacrifice. Jesus Christ stands here as High Priest, offering His Body and Blood for our sins, that we may venture to approach in spirit the throne of the awful majesty of God. Let us offer this sublime Sacrifice to God to render Him all the adoration, homage, awe, veneration and worship that are His due; to thank Him for His infinite attributes; to thank Him for the glory bestowed on His Divine Son, and for all that Jesus Christ has suffered for love of us; to thank Him for the glory of the sacred Humanity and for the graces and glory bestowed on the Blessed Virgin Mary and all the saints; to thank Him for all the graces bestowed on mankind especially on ourselves, who are so often ungrateful; and to beg new graces, above all the grace of final perseverance for ourselves and for all who are dear to us.

O Wonder of Wonders!

HOW solemn and sublime are the moments when the Sacred Host and the consecrated Chalice are raised aloft at Holy Mass! Songs of joy resound in the courts of heaven; the earth is visited with salvation; the souls in purgatory experience a mitigation of their pains; hell trembles and is afraid. Could we but behold what takes place upon our altars at the time of the Consecration, we should indeed tremble and stand in awe. The seraphic St. Francis of Assisi exclaims: "Let man be struck dumb, let the whole world tremble, the heavens themselves be amazed, when the Son of the living God lies upon the altar under the hands of the priest. O wonder of wonders! The only-begotten Son of God, the Lord of all creation, abases Himself so deeply that for man's salvation He deigns to conceal Himself under the form of a morsel of bread!"

When the moment comes for this incomparable mystery to take place, we may in spirit picture the gates of heaven rolled back, and the Son of God, clothed in majesty, descending in person to renew the work of our Redemption. We may visualize the choirs of angels going before Him in majesty and might, covering their faces and singing canticles of joy and exultation. St. Bridget describes how on one occasion she heard, at the time of the Consecration, the stars of the firmament and all the powers of heaven making sweet melody as they moved in their appointed courses. This harmony resounded far and wide. With it were mingled the voices of innumerable celestial spirits, chanting in tones of ineffable sweetness; the angelic choirs paid lowly reverence to the priest; the devils trembled with fear and fled in dismay.

Who can hear, without astonishment, of the preparation made in the celestial regions when the moment of the Consecration arrives in order that this wondrous miracle, this tremendous mystery, may be worthily celebrated! And yet we sinful mortals too often assist at the Divine Mysteries with little or no reverence, think little of their supernatural character, and regard the transubstantiation of the bread and wine as an ordinary, everyday occurrence!

St. Francis de Sales assures us that after the priest speaks the words of consecration and Jesus is present upon the altar, "He looks at us through the sacramental species as through a thin veil; He hears our prayers; His Heart is sensible to and feels our return of love, but also our indifference and lack of devotion."

Oh, may we enter fully into the spirit of Holy Mass, especially at the moment of the Consecration! Then we will be worthy of having fulfilled in us that blessed promise of our Savior to St. Gertrude: "It a person devoutly assists at Mass and carefully directs his attention to the Divine Victim, God the Father always regards such a one with complacency, in consideration of the delight He takes in the thrice sacred Host which is offered on the altar."

"Do This in Commemoration of Me!"

BY THESE words Jesus constituted His Apostles and their successors, who should be ordained by them, priests of the New Law, and conferred upon them the power of offering up the Sacrifice of the New Law, which is the Holy Mass. This the Catholic Church has always held and taught, and it is a doctrine of Faith defined by the Council of Trent: "If anyone shall say that by the words, *Do this in commemoration of Me*, Christ did not constitute the Apostles priests, and ordain that they and other priests should offer His Body and Blood, let him be anathema" (Sess. 22, Can. 2).

The commemoration or remembrance of Christ signified by these words is explained clearly by St. Paul when he adds: "For as often as you shall eat this Bread and drink the Cup, you shall proclaim the Death of the Lord until He come" (1 Cor. 11: 26). Holy Mass is a renewal of the Passion and Death of Our Lord and on that account alone it is a commemoration thereof. The

Church teaches: "Whosoever shall say that the Sacrifice of Mass is only a remembrance of the Sacrifice of the Cross, let him be anathema" (Council of Trent, Sess. 22). And in the same Session of the Council of Trent (Chap. 2) she teaches: "In this Divine Sacrifice which is celebrated in the Mass, that same Christ is contained and immolated in an unbloody manner who once offered Himself in a bloody manner on the altar of the Cross."

This remembrance should not be confined to a few simple thoughts or passing sentiments of tenderness, but should be deeply engraven in our hearts.

Seraphim cover their faces with their wings in presence of this august Mystery.

Hail, Victim Slain

Offering of the "Pure, Holy, and Immaculate Victim"
(First Prayer after the Consecration)

Having placed the Chalice on the altar and genuflected, the celebrant, standing erect with hands extended as at the Collect, says in secret or in an undertone, the prayer:

Unde et memores, Domine, nos servi tui, sed et plebs tua sancta, ejusdem Christi Filii tui Domini nostri, tam beatae passionis, necnon et ab inferis resurrectionis, sed et in coelos gloriosae ascensionis: offerimus praeclarae majestati tuae de tuis donis ac datis, hostiam ✠ *puram, hostiam* ✠ *sanctam, hostiam* ✠ *immaculatam, Panem* ✠ *sanctum vitae aeternae, et Calicem* ✠ *salutis perpetuae.*

Wherefore, O Lord, we Thy servants, as also Thy holy people, calling to mind the blessed Passion of the same Christ, Thy Son, Our Lord, His resurrection from hell, and glorious ascension into heaven, offer unto Thy most excellent majesty of Thine own gifts bestowed upon us, a pure ✠ Victim, a holy ✠ Victim, an immaculate ✠ Victim, the holy ✠ Bread of eternal life and the Chalice ✠ of everlasting salvation.

At the words "de tuis donis ac datis—of Thine own gifts bestowed upon us," the priest joins his hands, and when he says "Hostiam puram, Hostiam sanctam, Hostiam immaculatam — a pure Victim, a holy Victim, an immaculate Victim," he rests his left hand on the corporal, and with the right hand makes the Sign of the Cross, as indicated, three times over the Host and the Chalice together; then, at the words "Panem sanctum vitae aeternae—the holy Bread of eternal life," he signs the Host, and at "Calicem salutis perpetuae—the Chalice of everlasting salvation," he signs the Chalice.

CCORDING to the learned Father Sanchez, there is no part of the Mass which imparts to us greater consolation and spiritual joy than the prayer said by the priest immediately after the Elevation, when he offers the spotless Victim to God. The entire congregation shares in the offering of the Sacrifice. As members of God's Church, all the faithful are, in the words of St. Peter, "a royal priesthood," and this priestly character they exercise principally at the celebration of the Mass when they offer up the Body and Blood of Christ in closest union with the priest, and join to it their own sacrifices for the glory of God. They should make this offering by reciting the above prayer with attention and devotion.

The people of God are called "holy" because they are destined for holiness and adorned with sanctifying grace; because they are sanctified by the Holy Sacrifice and by the sprinkling of the Precious Blood shed upon them at the time of the elevation of the Chalice.

Faithful to the command of Christ: "Do this in commemoration of Me!" the priest and people now call to mind the Passion of Our Lord, by which we were redeemed, and also His resurrection and ascension, because through His sufferings He entered into glory, and these glorious mysteries form the completion and crown of the work of our Redemption. But, as Cardinal Bona remarks, it is not a mere commemoration of these mysteries, for the priest, at the same time offers to the Eternal Father the pure, the holy, the unspotted Host, the Body and Blood of Christ, which he still calls bread on account of the sacramental species; not, however, the bread which was there before the Consecration, but the Bread of eternal life and the Chalice of everlasting salvation.

The pure, holy, immaculate Victim offered up to the Divine Majesty is none other than the most pure Body, the most holy Soul and the immaculate Blood of Jesus, who is slain upon the altar, not by an actual and painful, but by a supernatural and mystical immolation. The sacred Humanity of Christ is the true holocaust, which He Himself, in His Divine nature, offers at the same time as the priest and each one of the faithful present who unites with the priest in making the oblation. This offering is so precious that it exceeds in value the whole world with all its treasures; it is a treasure so costly that it outweighs the vast heavens and all their infinite riches; for the Humanity of Christ is so noble, so sacred, that nothing equal to

It has ever been or ever will be created by the hand of God. This offering, therefore, causes infinite gratification to the Most Holy Trinity, and God becomes, as it were, our debtor, for what we offer Him is worth infinitely more than what we owe Him.

This oblation is called *pure* in contradistinction to the sacrifices of the Gentiles, which were impure and corrupt; *holy*, in contradistinction to the sacrifices of the Old Law, which were not holy in the sense that they could of themselves impart sanctity, as does our Sacrifice, which takes away the sins of the world. It is called *immaculate*, because Christ, who is now present under the consecrated Species, is the innocent Lamb of God who takes away the sins of the world, through whom and through whose merits alone men are sanctified. As the priests of the Old Law, by eating of the sacrifices which they offered, sustained their earthly life, so Christians, by eating and drinking of this holy Sacrifice and Sacrament, are sustained and strengthened in their spiritual and supernatural life.

St. Thomas tells us that, after the Consecration the priest does not make the Sign of the Cross for the purpose of blessing or consecrating, but to commemorate the virtue and power of the Cross and the manner of Christ's death. The Church omits nothing that may serve to remind the priest and the people that the Sacrifice of the Altar is the same as the Sacrifice of the Cross, and hence the Sign of the Cross is so often repeated.

The Most Acceptable Oblation
(Second Prayer after the Consecration)

Having blessed the oblation, the priest extends his hands and continues:

Supra quae propitio ac sereno vultu respicere digneris: et accepta habere, sicuti accepta habere dignatus es munera pueri tui justi Abel, et sacrificium patriarchae nostri Abrahae, et quod tibi obtulit summus sacerdos tuus Melchisedech sanctum sacrificium, immaculatam hostiam.	Upon which do Thou vouchsafe to look with a propitious and serene countenance, and to accept them, as Thou wert graciously pleased to accept the gifts of Thy just servant Abel, and the sacrifice of our patriarch Abraham, and that which Thy high priest Melchisedech offered to Thee, a holy sacrifice, a spotless victim.

THE Body and Blood of Jesus Christ are infinitely more pleasing to God than were all the sacrifices of the Old Law. This prayer does not, therefore, refer to the Sacrifice itself of Christ's Body and Blood, but rather to the priest and the people who are offering Christ's Sacrifice to God. The purer our life and the more perfect our disposition, the more pleasing will our offering be.

Holy Scripture says of the sacrifice of Abel: "The Lord had respect to Abel and to his offerings" (Gen. 4: 4). He regarded the heart and disposition of him who offered the gift, and because these were good, the gifts pleased Him. The same principle applies to the Eucharistic Sacrifice, since Christ offers Himself on the altar through our ministration. Pure and precious though the Sacrifice is in itself, God will accept it more readily if it is offered by pure and holy hands. With reason, therefore, do we entreat God not to spurn the Eucharistic offering in our unworthy hands.

At the Offertory we offered ourselves, body and soul, senses and faculties, our works, prayers, desires and needs; we placed ourselves in spirit upon the paten beside the host as a living sacrifice with Jesus Christ. This union, was symbolized by the mingling of the water and wine. We, ourselves, therefore, are part of the offering, and this sense of our own unworthiness prompts us to beseech God to look with mercy upon our sacrifice. In order to sacrifice ourselves worthily with Jesus we should have His dispositions, His purity and sanctity, in which virtues, we are, alas, so deficient, and for which we must substitute a heartfelt humility.

WHEN THE ANGELS INTERCEDE
(Third Prayer after the Consecration)

Supplices te rogamus, omnipotens Deus: Jube haec perferri per manus sancti Angeli tui in sublime altare tuum, in conspectu divinae majestatis tuae; ut quotquot, ex hac altaris participatione, sacrosanctum Filii tui, Corpus ✠ et San ✠ guinem sumpserimus, omni benedictione coelesti, et gratia repleamur. Per eumdem Christum Dominum nostrum. Amen.	We most humbly beseech Thee, Almighty God, to command that these things be borne by the hands of Thy holy Angel to Thine altar on high, in the sight of Thy Divine Majesty, that as many of us as at this altar shall partake of and receive the most holy Body ✠ and ✠ Blood of Thy Son may be filled with every heavenly blessing and grace. Through the same Christ our Lord. Amen.

THIS prayer contains a mysterious request: that God may cause our offering to be carried by His angel to His altar on high, in the presence of His Divine Majesty, so that by partaking of the sacrificial food we may be filled with heavenly blessings. There is no altar in heaven, properly speaking, because there is no real sacrifice, as on earth. Our Divine Savior forever stands before the face of God as our High Priest; presenting to the Divine Majesty His Wounds and His bloody Death, in order to implore grace and mercy for us. In like manner, unceasing sacrifices of praise, thanksgiving, atonement and petition rise from the heart of our Blessed Mother and from all the angels and saints to the Triune God. The Hearts of Jesus and Mary, glowing with love, may, therefore, be said to constitute the "altar on high" upon which the most perfect sacrifice of praise is uninterruptedly offered to God.

When the Church, asks that "our sacrifice may be carried to the altar on high," she seeks to unite it with the Divine praise in heaven; she entreats God to permit our poor, imperfect worship to become united with the homage of the Church Triumphant, so that by this union all the faithful who receive Holy Communion at this Mass, either really or spiritually, may share in the fullest blessing of heaven. Our faith in the Communion of Saints is beautifully expressed in this prayer, and by the kiss which the priest here imparts upon the altar stone where the relics of the saints repose.

The word *angel* in this prayer is given various interpretations. A first group of liturgists maintains that it is to be taken in its ordinary sense. But among these, some take it in a general sense without specifying any particular angel, whereas others attempt to identify the angel as the Angel of the Eucharist; the Angel of Baptism and Penance; the Angel of Christian prayer; the Archangel Michael, the prince of the heavenly hosts; or even the guardian angel of the priest. Others hold that this angel is none other than our Lord Jesus Christ Himself, the "Angel of the Great Council," who presents the oblation of Himself at the throne of the Divinity. Still another group maintains that the word angel here signifies the Holy Spirit. However, the weight of historical evidence seems to favor the first of these interpretations as being the traditional one. It is certain, according to Christian tradition, that angels are present around the altar during the celebration of Mass. Some of the Fathers make reference especially to angels commissioned to carry our prayers and sacrifices before the throne of God.

Besides the guardian angels of the faithful who are present, thousands of celestial spirits assist at Mass, reverently worshiping their Lord and God. It was revealed to St. Mechtilde that three thousand angels from the seventh choir, the Thrones, are ever in devout attendance around every tabernacle where the Blessed Sacrament is reserved. Doubtless a much greater number are present at Holy Mass, which is not merely a sacrament but also a sacrifice. Hence, it is not lowly mortals alone who call upon God: the angels prostrate before Him, the archangels plead in behalf of men. The angels are inflamed with the love of God; they behold Him face to face. Consequently they obtain what they ask of God more readily than we do by our cold, careless petitions, so full of distractions. It is fitting, therefore, that we place our offerings and our petitions in the pure hands of the angels, to be presented to the Most High, that He may receive them graciously and pardon our indevotion for the sake of the devotion of the celestial spirits with whom we associate ourselves.

Both the actions of the priest and the signs employed by him have a mystical significance. He joins his hands, bows his head and bends low to signify the profound humility of Christ hanging upon the Cross and praying for us, and to signify also his own humility, by which, being impressed with his own unworthiness of so great a ministry, he implores that his prayer and sacrifice may be presented to God by an angel. He kisses the altar, by which is signified that Christ, hanging upon the Cross, enduring the anguish of death, ceased not to embrace in the bonds of charity all men for whose salvation He thirsted. The priest makes the Sign of the Cross three times — once over the Host, once over the Chalice and once on himself; by which is represented that the torments which Christ endured in His Flesh and which He suffered in the effusion of His Blood, profit and always will benefit both priest and people to eternal salvation if only they embrace

Multitudes of angels surround the altar in adoring love during the celebration of Holy Mass. (St. Jolm Chrysostom)

the Cross of Christ; for it is through the Cross that we are replenished with every grace and heavenly blessing.

By the words concluding the prayer, *"Per eumdem Christum Dominum nostrum*—Through the same Christ our Lord," at which the priest rejoins his hands, we are reminded of Christ upon the Cross in the sight of His Heavenly Father, enduring the reproaches, the blasphemies and opprobriums of men, that He might enrich us with all spiritual gifts and graces. Let us, therefore, at this moment implore an abundance of supernatural graces and heavenly aid through our Lord and Savior Jesus Christ.

Unfailing Succor of the Departed
(Memento for the Dead)

AFTER the foregoing prayers of oblation, the Church turns in pitying love to her captive children in purgatory and supplicates the Divine mercy in their behalf.

When beginning the *"Memento etiam. . . ,"* the priest slowly separates his hands but joins them at the words *"in somno pacis,"* —an indication of peace and rest. He then raises them to his face, inclines his head, and fixing his eyes upon the Sacred Host prays for the departed. He then raises his head, holds his hands extended, and continues the prayer. At the *"Per eumdem..."* he again joins his hands.

Memento etiam, Domine, famulorum famularumque tuarum N. et N. qui nos praecesserunt cum signo fidei, et dormiunt in somno pacis.	Be mindful, O Lord, of Thy servants and handmaids N. and N., who are gone before us with the sign of faith, and sleep in the sleep of peace.
Ipsis, Domine, et omnibus in Christo quiescentibus, locum refrigerii, lucis et pacis, ut indulgeas, deprecamur. Per eumdem Christum Dominum nostrum. Amen.	To these, O Lord, and to all that rest in Christ, we beseech Thee, grant a place of refreshment, light, and peace. Through the same Christ our Lord. Amen.

It may be noted that at the concluding formula of this prayer, "Through Christ our Lord," the priest not only joins his hands, but also bows his head. The inclination of the head at this point and at these words is singular, as otherwise it is nowhere prescribed when the name of "Christ" occurs without the addition of *Jesus*. The reason for it must, therefore, be grounded on the text of the prayer itself and have some mysterious signification. When dying, Christ bowed His head on the Cross and then descended into the depths of the kingdom of the dead, there to console the just who lived previous to His coming and to deliver them from their captivity. This the priest would now call to mind by bowing his head, since he here prays and implores for all who rest in Christ that the atoning Blood, flowing from the Eucharistic Sacrifice as from a fountain, may flow into purgatory to alleviate and shorten the sufferings of the poor souls therein detained.

Holy Mass is the sacrifice of the whole Church: the Church in heaven, the Church on earth and the Church in purgatory. The Church on earth is a most tender Mother. In her maternal solicitude she does not forget to pray for those who have departed this life. This strengthens our faith in the Communion of Saints and brings unspeakable relief to the members committed to expiation in the Church Suffering. Near the most solemn part of Holy Mass, when the Divine Victim is being immolated upon the altar, Holy Church bids us remember those who have gone before us, signed with the sign of faith, the indelible mark of baptism, and who rest in the sleep of peace. We pray for all the souls in purgatory, for all of whom we ask a place of refreshment, having reference to the fire with which they are tormented; a place of light, referring to the darkness in which they are enveloped; a place of peace, referring to the anxieties and troubles which disturb them. We then beg for succor and relief for those holy souls from the threefold species of suffering by which the Justice of God expiates their sins and purifies them for eternal beatitude.

The Treasures of the Mass

The Church in heaven, in purgatory and on earth is united in Holy Mass.

There are many different ways of helping the suffering souls and of delivering them from purgatory; but none of these is so sure and so effectual as the holy Sacrifice of the Mass. The Church, speaking by the Council of Trent, declares: "This Ecumenical Synod teaches that the souls detained in purgatory are helped by the suffrages of the faithful, but principally by the acceptable Sacrifice of the Altar" (Sess. 25). St. Thomas asserted the same three centuries previously: "By no other oblation can the souls in purgatory be more speedily released than by the Sacrifice of the Mass."

COMMEMORATION OF THE CHURCH MILITANT
(Nobis Quoque Peccatoribus)

The priest now places his left hand on the corporal while he strikes his breast "with the right and says in an audible voice the first three words of the following prayer "nobis quoque peccatoribus." He then extends his hands at the words: "Per Christum Dominum nostrum."

Nobis quoque peccatoribus, famulis tuis, de multitudine miserationum tuarum sperantibus, partem aliquam et societatem donare digneris, cum tuis sanctis Apostolis et Martyribus: cum Joanne, Stephano, Matthia, Barnaba, Ignatio, Alexandro, Marcellino, Petro, Felicitate, Perpetua, Agatha, Lucia Agnete Caecilia, Anastasia et onmibus sanctis tuis: intra quorum nos consortium, non aestimator meriti, sed veniae, quaesumus, largitor admitte. Per Christum Dominum nostrum. Per quem haec omnia, Domine, semper bona creas, sanctificas, vivificas, benedicis, et praestas nobis. Per ip ✠ *sum, et cum ip* ✠ *so, et in ip* ✠ *so, est tibi Deo*

To us sinners, also, Thy servants hoping in the multitude of Thy mercies, vouchsafe to grant some part and fellowship with Thy holy Apostles and Martyrs: with John, Stephen, Matthias, Barnabas, Ignatius, Alexander, Marcellinus, Peter Felicitas, Perpetua, Agatha, Lucy, Agnes, Caecilia, Anastasia and with all Thy saints, into whose company we pray Thee to admit us, not considering our merit, but of Thine own free pardon. Through Christ our Lord; through whom, O Lord, Thou dost create, hallow, quicken and bless these Thine ever-bountiful gifts and give them to us. Through ✠ Him, and with ✠ Him, and in ✠ Him, is to Thee, God the Father ✠

Patri ✠ *omnipotenti, in unitate Spiritus* ✠ *sancti, omnis honor et gloria.*	Almighty, in the unity of the Holy ✠ Ghost, all honor and glory.

MANY who were present at the death of Christ on the Cross and saw the wonders which took place, contritely struck their breasts and confessed the Divinity of Christ. Like them, and like the penitent thief on the cross, we, too, confess our sins and grieve over our offenses. We call ourselves "God's servants" because redeemed by Christ's Blood; we beg for participation, with the saints enumerated and with all the saints, in the eternal joys of heaven. The priest and the faithful strike their breasts after having beheld the mysteries which have here taken place. The stream of grace of the Holy Sacrifice has already been poured out upon the Church Suffering, and now the priest prays that the Church Militant may also have a share in the same. But since only repentant and contrite hearts will be granted this participation, he strikes his breast and acknowledges himself a sinner, and, in his person, also the faithful who are present.

With a loud voice he cries to the Lord from the depths of his heart, and calls upon those present to unite their plea with his. The principal prayer of the petition is that by this Holy Sacrifice the Church Suffering and the Church Militant may be admitted into the Church Triumphant.

In this prayer, mention is made of the holy Apostles and Martyrs, fifteen in all (eight male and seven female saints). These represent the several orders and states of personages in the Church. St. John Baptist is of the order of Prophets, St. Stephen of the order of Deacons, St. Matthias of the order of Apostles; St. Barnabas was a Levite; St. Ignatius of Antioch is of the order of Bishops; St. Alexander I was a martyr-Pope; St. Marcellinus is of the order of priests; St. Peter, the fellow-martyr of St. Marcellinus, was an exorcist, and is of the order of Clerks. SS. Perpetua and Felicitas are of the Married state; SS. Agatha, Lucy, Agnes and Cecilia are all of the state of Virgins; and St. Anastasia is ranked among Widows. The saints mentioned are those who in Rome, the principal city of Christendom, were at all times held in great veneration.

After the priest has thus assembled the Church Suffering and the Church Triumphant with the Church Militant around the Sacrifice of Christ, he continues, while he signs the Eucharistic Forms with the Sign of the Cross: *"Per Christum Dominum nostrum. Per quem haec omnia, Domine, semper bona creas, sanctificas, vivificas, benedicis, et praestas nobis*—Through Christ our Lord; through whom, O Lord, Thou dost create, hallow, quicken and bless these Thine ever-bountiful gifts and give them to us."

Thus he draws all creation into the sacred circle of the Sacrifice, signifying that by this holy Eucharistic Sacrifice of Christ all other gifts which God gives us for body and soul, yes, all creatures, are blessed and sanctified.

"Through Him, and with Him and in Him"
(Minor Elevation)

At the words "et praestas nobis" the priest uncovers the Chalice, placing the pall on the veil or against the altar card. He then genuflects and immediately after takes the Host between the thumb and forefinger of his right hand, and makes the Sign of the Cross with It three times over the Chalice, while he prays "per ipsum, et cum ipso et in ipso"; then he makes the Sign of the Cross with the Host twice over the corporal in front of the Chalice, at the words "est tibi Deo Patri omnipotenti, in unitate Spiritus Sancti." Then, holding the Host over the Chalice with his right hand, and holding the Chalice with his left, he elevates it a little together with the Host, saying the words "omnis honor et gloria." He then places the Chalice on the corporal, also the Host, and purifies his fingers over the Chalice before covering it with the pall.

ALL honor and glory is given to God the Father *through* the Son, *with* the Son, and *in* the Son, and in the unity of the Holy Ghost, who, proceeding from the other two Persons, is equally adored, praised and honored with Them forever. Thus, by virtue of our union with the Divine Victim on our altars, we, poor, insignificant creatures, can give all honor and glory to God! There is no longer any stain or deficiency in our homage, for we give it through Jesus, with Jesus and in Jesus, who loves, honors and glorifies the Father in an infinite measure; and He—oh, grace of our Redeemer and Head! — by making use of us poor instruments, gives to our homage a Divine character. We are creatures, and our first duty to our Creator is adoration, worship and praise, but of ourselves we could never offer this homage in a worthy manner. Therefore the Heavenly Father has given us His adorable Son to be our Savior, our Divine Victim, that *through* Him, *with* Him, and *in* Him we can return, to the Heavenly Father all honor and glory. What joy, that we can return to the Heavenly Father as much as He gives to us!

At these words of praise, the priest makes the Sign of the Cross three times over the Chalice with the Sacred Host, to indicate the union of the Body and Blood, of Christ in the eternal beatitude in which He now glorifies the Father and the Holy Ghost and is Himself glorified by the other two Divine Persons. He then makes the Sign of the Cross twice between the Chalice and his breast, to indicate our union with Christ and His praise. At the last words, he slightly raises the Chalice, holding the Sacred Host above it, thus symbolically raising up to God the praise-offering of Christ, as the praise-offering of the entire Church.

The lifting up of the Chalice together with the Sacred Host further indicates that by this Holy Sacrifice all creation has again been raised up to God from whom it had been separated by sin. It is also symbolic of the ascension of Our Lord; for, just as the ascension ended His priestly career, His sacrifice on earth, and commenced His royal activity, the government of the Church, so this ceremony closes the priestly or sacrificial part of the Mass and introduces the kingly part.

Furthermore, Christ does not confine Himself to pleading from the altar for all who are present, but, to enhance the potency of His prayer, He sacrifices Himself to God on their behalf. He makes an oblation of Himself in a manner so unspeakably sublime that the highest powers of heaven are incapable of fully comprehending it. What, then, can be more pleasing to the Heavenly Father, or more salutary for our welfare, than to unite ourselves in fullest confidence with the Sacred Victim upon the altar, and to pray with all the fervor and devotion of our hearts: *"Through Him and with Him and in Him be to Thee, God the Father Almighty, in the unity of the Holy Ghost all honor and glory"*?

The praise-offering of Christ, our Head, is an everlasting one, and therefore the priest closes this eulogy with the words: *"Per omnia saecula saeculorum—*For ever and ever," to which the faithful give their assent by the response: "*Amen!* —So be it!"

This marks the conclusion of the Canon of the Mass.

The Breaking of Bread

AS THE *Preface* terminates the *Offertory* and introduces the Canon, so the Pater Noster seals the Canon, as it were, and introduces the liturgical devotion for Holy Communion. With this solemn liturgical prayer, the transition is made from the sacrifice-offering to the sacrifice-banquet. The Our Father is the table prayer of God's children gathered about the altar-table to receive their daily Bread.

The receiving of the Heavenly Bread, union with God and fellow-men in the bond of charity and forgiveness, security from evil in Christ, all are comprised in the one dominant note of this portion of the Mass: peace. Peace is the characteristic note of the sacrifice-banquet, as praise is that of the sacrifice-offering. Thus the two great purposes of all the liturgy are fulfilled: the honoring of God and the sanctification of man, through Christ. Peace among men is the fruit of that good will which first gives glory to God.

The Breaking of Bread

Pater Noster

The celebrant, having placed the Chalice and Host on the altar at the words concluding the prayer, "Nobis quoque peccatoribus — Also to us sinners...," covers the Chalice with the pall, genuflects, rests his hands on the corporal and says aloud: "Per omnia saecula saeculorum—forever and ever." He then joins his hands at the "Oremus" and bows his head to the Blessed Sacrament, keeping his hands joined while he says the introductory prayer and then continues with the *Pater Noster*:

Praeceptis salutaribus moniti, et divina institutione formati, audemus dicere:	Taught by the precepts of salvation, and following the Divine commandment, we make bold to say:
Pater noster, qui es in coelis, sanctificetur nomen tuum: adveniat regnum tuum: fiat voluntas tua, sicut in coelo et in terra: panem nostrum quotidianum da nobis hodie et dimitte nobis debita nostra, sicut et nos dimittimus debitoribus nostris: et ne nos inducas in tentationem.	Our Father, who art in heaven, hallowed be Thy Name; Thy kingdom come; Thy will be done on earth as it is in heaven. Give us this day our daily bread: and forgive us our trespasses, as we forgive those who trespass against us. And lead us not into temptation.
℟. *Sed libera nos a malo.*	℟. But deliver us from evil.
℣. *Amen.*	℣. Amen.

When the priest begins the "Pater Noster," which is said aloud, he extends his hands and keeps them in that position till the "Et ne nos inducas—And lead us not..." During the recital of the "Pater Noster," the priest keeps his eyes fixed on the Sacred Host. When the acolyte answers, "Sed libera nos a malo—But deliver us from evil," the celebrant responds "Amen," in an undertone.

BEING the prayer composed by Our Lord Himself, and the model of all prayers, the *Pater Noster* should naturally form a part of the liturgy of the Mass. It occupies the present place, no doubt, for the reason that it was the last prayer taught in the early Church to the catechumens before baptism, because the Church wished them to be imbued with the spirit of faith before imparting to them Our Lord's own prayer. This was done both out of reverence for the prayer, and because the prayer is one which embodies all the petitions necessary for salvation and implies all the dispositions which the Christian soul should possess.

This prayer is said during Holy Mass at the part when both priest and people should desire most earnestly that the fruits of the Holy Sacrifice and of Holy Communion may be applied to their souls. In union with our Divine Savior, and thinking of Him as He was dying upon the Cross, we renew our humility and confidence by saying: "*Praeceptis salutaribus moniti, et divina institutione formati, audemus dicere* — Taught by the precepts of salvation, and following the Divine commandment, we make bold to say:"—

"*Pater noster, qui es in coelis*—Our Father, who art in heaven," who art glorious and exalted forever in the heaven of heavens. "*Sanctificetur nomen tuum* — Hallowed be Thy Name!"—May Thy holy and ineffable Name be acknowledged, adored and glorified by all people and nations. "*Adveniat regnum tuum*—Thy kingdom come" now by Thy grace and hereafter by Thy glory, that Thou mayest always reign over our hearts, and that we may always be subject to Thee. "*Fiat voluntas tua, sicut in coelo et in terra* — Thy will be done on earth as it is in heaven." — May that holy will be done by us, and in us, and in all that concerns us and Thy creatures. "*Panem nostrum quotidianum da nobis hodie*—Give us this day our daily bread," both spiritual and temporal, and especially grant that we may worthily receive that supernatural Bread which is the spiritual nourishment of our souls, the Body and Blood of Thy only-begotten Son, our Lord Jesus Christ; grant that we may always hope and rely upon Thy Providence, and use worthily and properly all Thy gifts and graces.

"*Et dimitte nobis debita nostra, sicut et nos dimittimus debitoribus nostris* — And forgive us our trespasses, as we forgive those who trespass against us." Through Thy infinite mercy and love, and the merits of Thy Divine Son, pardon all our sins and offenses; grant us Thy help, that from our hearts we may forgive all our enemies and all who in any way have offended and injured us, that we may say with Thy Divine Son, who prayed for all His enemies upon the Cross, "Father, forgive them, for they know not what they do." Thus prepared by charity and love, may we receive His Sacred Body and Blood and participate in all the fruits of the adorable Sacrifice. "*Et ne nos inducas in tentationem*—And lead us not into temptation."—Protect us against all the attacks and temptations of the world, the flesh and the devil, that we may repel and overcome them. "*Sed libera nos a malo*—But deliver us from evil," from the evils of guilt, of punishment and all the calamities and evils consequent on our sins. Amen.

The celebrant raises his voice at the *Oremus* and *Pater Noster*, after the secret prayer of the *Canon*. During the *Canon* he has, as it were, entered into the Holy of Holies, there to commune alone with God. This silence may be considered as commemorating those awful hours during which Our Lord hung upon the Cross and bore in silence the scoff's and blasphemies of the Jewish multitude, and silently prayed for all His enemies to His Heavenly Father. The *Pater Noster,* which contains seven petitions, is recited aloud to remind the faithful of the seven last words which our Savior spoke in a loud voice when hanging on the Cross.

A Solemn Compact

A MOST necessary disposition for reciting the "Our Father" worthily, not only during Holy Mass, but at all times, is the spirit of forgiveness, for in it we pray: *Forgive us our trespasses, as we forgive those who trespass against us.* This is a solemn compact made with God: Do Thou forgive me my sins as I forgive the offenses of others," "Turn away Thy face from my sins," we ask of the Almighty. He will assuredly do so if we forgive the shortcomings of others, forget their misdeeds and refuse to let the thought of injury rankle in our heart. To forgive one's enemies is a genuine Christian act. Discontent, revenge, even hatred, are rife in the world today. If everyone after the Consecration would conform his sentiments to these Divine words, there would be more peace and harmony among those who call themselves Christians.

Have we ever realized that Christ makes as the one condition of our being forgiven ourselves, our own forgiveness of others? "With what measure you measure, it shall be measured to you again" (Matt. 7: 2).

Of all passions, hatred and revenge have the deadliest consequences for both soul and body. Envy and hatred destroy all the beauty and peace of life and of our immortal soul. A real Christian, a follower of Christ, will forgive from his heart, will forget the past absolutely. In no other disposition can one truthfully say the "Lord's Prayer." Otherwise, we simply lie to the all-knowing God when we harbor ill-feelings or hatred in our heart. While reciting this most sacred of prayers, let us promise Our Lord to forgive; if people have been unkind or injurious to us, let us forget it, wipe it out of our mind and heart entirely with one act of generosity. That is what our Savior has done for us times without number; that, too, is one of the graces He gives us in Holy Mass—the grace of peace and good will.

All should be attentive to recite the "Pater Noster" during Holy Mass at the same time as it is prayed by the priest. Though we should recite it many times during the day, it has incomparably more value in the sight of God when we pray it at Holy Mass with the priest because the priest says this prayer in union with the Divine Savior who is Himself the Priest

THE BREAKING OF BREAD

and Victim of the adorable Sacrifice. This prayer has a special value. It contains seven petitions, the first three of which refer directly to God, the last four to ourselves. We should say this prayer: through Jesus, with Jesus and in Jesus, who is immolating Himself on the altar for us, and seek at the same time to animate our hearts with the spirit of these Divine words.

SUPPLICATION FOR PEACE
(Libera)

> The celebrant, resting his left hand on the corporal, with his right hand withdraws the paten from under it and cleanses or wipes it with the purificator, bringing the left hand to assist in holding the paten if necessary. Afterwards he places ths purificator in a convenient place to his right hand side on the altar, with the concave side towards the corporal, whilst he says the "Libera" in secret. At the name of the Blessed Virgin he bows his head. Before he says "da propitius —mercifully grant..." he raises his left hand from the corporal, and places it on his breast. With the paten he makes on himself the Sign of the Cross at the words "da propitius," and kisses the paten at the word "pacem" to remind himself and the faithful that it was by the Cross Christ became "our peace." Whilst continuing the prayer to the end, the celebrant puts the Sacred Host on the paten with the forefinger of the left hand and places the paten, with the Host upon it, on the corporal, resting it on the foot of the chalice. Then, laying his left hand on the base of the chalice, he takes off the pall, and placing his hands on the altar, he genuflects.

Libera nos, quaesumus Domine, ab omnibus malis praeteritis, praesentibus, et futuris, et intercedente beata et gloriosa semper Virgine Dei genitrice Maria, cum beatis Apostolis tuis Petro et Paulo, atque Andrea, et omnibus sanctis, da propitius pacem in diebus nostris: ut ope misericordiae tuae adjuti, et a peccato simus semper liberi, et ab omni perturbatione securi. Per eumdem Dominum nostrum Jesum Christum Filium tuum, qui tecum vivit et regnat in unitate Spiritus sancti Deus. Per omnia saecula saeculorum. Amen.

Deliver us, we beseech Thee, O Lord, from all evils, past, present and to come; and by the intercession of the blessed and glorious Mary ever Virgin, Mother of God, together with Thy blessed Apostles Peter and Paul, and Andrew, and all the saints, mercifully grant peace in our days: that through the help of Thy mercy we may always be free from sin and from all trouble. Through the same Jesus Christ Thy Son, our Lord, who liveth and reigneth with Thee in the unity of the Holy Ghost, one God. Forever and ever. ℟. Amen.

THE *Libera nos*, which follows the last petition of the Lord's Prayer, is a continuation and enlargement of the "Pater Noster." In it we pray God to deliver us from all evils: past —our sins, for which we beg forgiveness; present— temptations and frailties, that we may overcome and conquer them; future—that we may obtain grace to preserve us from falling again, and be fortified against impending dangers.

These graces are asked through the intercession of the Blessed Virgin Mary, who stood at the foot of the Cross, and whose soul was pierced by the sword of sorrow; through the intercession of St. Peter, the prince of the Apostles, who for his Divine Master and like Him "was crucified, but with his head downwards, out of humility; through the intercession of St. Paul, who could say: "I bear the marks of Our Lord Jesus in my body" (Gal. 6: 17); through the intercession of St. Andrew, whom Christ called to be His first disciple and who likewise suffered martyrdom upon a cross. Through these and through the intercession of all the saints, saved by the merits of the Cross, we beg of the Divine Mercy peace, that we may be always free from sin and secure against all disturbances: and all these supplications are made through the same Jesus Christ, our Lord.

Our Lord is called, in Holy Scripture, "The Prince of Peace." True to this noble title He has been from the beginning and will be to the end of the world an ambassador of peace. On the day of His birth His mission of peace was proclaimed to the world by His angels: "Glory to God in the highest and peace on earth, among men of good will" (Luke 2: 14). From the crib to the Cross, throughout His public life. He went about preaching the good tidings of peace. He taught His Apostles to greet every house they visited with the words "Peace to this house" (Luke 10: 6). Just before His death, when He delivered His parting address to His Apostles, He said, "Peace I leave with you, My peace I give to you" (John 14: 27). And after His glorious resurrection the first greeting of our risen Savior to His Apostles was again a message of peace. Peace was His word of salutation. It was His blessing. It was His legacy.

Our Lord wants all mankind in every age and country to be partakers of His peace. But in what does this peace consist? The peace of Our Lord consists, first of all, in a good conscience. It is that quiet sense of security existing in the soul, produced by the faithful accomplishment of our duties, the keeping of God's commandments. It is that tranquillity of soul which characterized the martyrs, who underwent the most atrocious tortures with an admirable serenity.

Our Lord wishes to establish in our hearts a triple peace: First, peace with God, by the observance of His precepts; secondly, peace with our neighbor, by the practice of those two beautiful social virtues: justice and charity; and thirdly, peace with our own selves, by controlling our passions and evil inclinations, keeping them subject to right reason, and keeping our reason in harmony with the law of God.

Peace is the fruit of victory and victory will be ours only after the fight. We must therefore buckle on the armor of Christ, the Cross, arm ourselves with the grace of God and fight manfully. Life is a warfare. We must wage incessant war against the enemies of our soul—the world, the flesh and the devil. Then and only then shall we enjoy the true peace of Christ, the peace that surpasses all understanding, that peace which the world cannot give.

The means of acquiring this peace are twofold. First and foremost, we must remove from our soul that which disturbs or destroys our peace, namely sin. Sin is that loathsome venom which stifles the conscience, darkens the intellect and finally takes away the supernatural life of our soul. Venial sin disturbs our peace, while a single mortal sin is sufficient to destroy it entirely and perhaps forever. Therefore, our first duty is to acquire this peace by sincere contrition and a good confession. Then, we must not only acquire peace, but must preserve it intact. For this purpose we must fortify the citadel of our soul by prayer and the frequent reception of the sacraments. If we make use of these two means, the victory in the combat is assured. Then the Prince of peace will reign in our hearts and give us even here below a foretaste of the eternal bliss of heaven.

From the offering of the Host to this part of the Mass, the paten remains hidden under the corporal at Low Mass, or under the humeral veil at solemn High Mass. The explanation of this, as given by Pope Benedict XIV, is that during that time it is not wanted for use and is therefore placed in a convenient position or taken away and covered, to keep it free from dust or from being soiled in any way. At the *Libera* it is brought forth by the celebrant, or, at solemn High Mass, handed to him by the subdeacon, because he now requires it for the ceremonies of the Mass.

In a mystical sense, the placing of the paten under the corporal, or covering it with the veil, signifies the Divinity of Our Lord, which remained veiled and hidden from the eyes of men and of His own disciples during the time of His Passion, but immediately after His Death revealed itself, so that men, seeing the sun darkened, together with other wondrous signs of the Divine power and majesty, went down from Calvary striking their breasts and saying; Truly, this Man was the Son of God (Mark 15: 39).

The Breaking of Bread

The Breaking of the Sacred Host

  After genuflecting, the celebrant moves the Sacred Host with the forefinger of his left hand to one end of the paten. Then, taking It between the thumb and forefinger of both hands, he breaks It reverently over the Chalice, into two equal parts, saying at the same time the words, "Per eumdem Dominum nostrum Jesum Christum Filium tuum—Through the same Jesus Christ, Thy Son, our Lord." He places upon the paten the half of the Sacred Host which he holds in his right hand, and from the half retained in the left he breaks from the lower part a small portion, saying at the same time, "qui tecum vivit et regnat—who liveth and reigneth with Thee." Holding this portion of the Sacred Host in his right hand, he places that which is in his left beside the other half on the paten, saying the words, "in unitate Spiritus Sancti Deus— in the unity of the Holy Ghost." Then holding the particle of the Host which he retains in his right hand over the Chalice, and with his left hand holding the Chalice (per nodum) he says aloud, "Per omnia saecula saeculorum—World without end," to which the acolyte answers, "Amen." With the same particle he then makes the Sign of the Cross three times over the Chalice, saying the words:

Pax ✠ Domini sit ✠ semper vobis- ✠ cum.	The peace ✠ of the Lord be ✠ always with ✠ you

  The acolyte having answered, "Et cum spiritu tuo—And with thy spirit," the celebrant lowers the small particle into the Chalice, saying at the same time in secret:

Haec commixtio et consecratio Corporis et Sanguinis Domini nostri Jesu Christi, fiat accipientibus nobis in vitam aeternam. Amen.	May this mingling and consecration of the Body and Blood of our Lord Jesus Christ avail us who receive It unto life everlasting. Amen.

  The priest having finished this prayer, rubs his fingers over the Chalice so that any very small particle adhering to them may fall into it, and then, laying his left hand on the base of the Chalice, he covers it with the pall and genuflects.

So important is this rite of the fraction of the Host that the bishop after the ceremony of ordination urges the newly-ordained priests to study carefully the entire rite of the Mass before they celebrate, especially the Consecration, the Fraction and the Communion.

Christ broke the bread before He gave it to His disciples to eat at the Last Supper. The Apostles retained the custom, and as a result, the whole Eucharistic celebration among the first Christians was called "The Breaking of Bread" (Acts 2: 42; 20: 7,11). The breaking of the Host at Mass is a ceremony of deep significance. By the breaking of the Sacred Host is signified the separation of the Body and Soul of Christ at the moment of His Death.

According to Catholic doctrine, Christ, whole and entire, is present both under the species or accidents of bread and under the species or accidents of wine. It is also a dogma of faith that He is whole and entire under every part or portion of the species when separated; and it is theologically certain that He is whole and entire under every part of the species even when the species remain united, no separation of them being made. Then, too, it is a doctrine of our Faith that the Body of Christ is now glorious, immortal and impassible, and that It cannot be in any real sense broken or mutilated.

Sacred writers discover in this action a deeply symbolical and mystical signification, and suggest many thoughts and sentiments for devotion and edification:—

(1) There were three things in Christ which in His Passion and Death were separated—namely His Blood, His Body and His Soul. First, in His Passion, His Blood was separated from His Body; then, in His Death, His Body was separated from His Soul. These three were separated in the Passion and Death of Christ, although the Divine-Person remained always united with the Soul, the Body and the Blood. By the first fraction of the Host, therefore, into two parts, we are reminded of the separation of the Blood of Christ from His Body. The second fraction, by which a small particle is separated from the larger half, represents the separation of the Soul of Christ from His Body.

(2) Again, these fractions are made over the Chalice, because the separation of Body, Blood and Soul of

Christ took place when He was hanging upon the Cross. Two parts of the Host are placed upon the paten, by which is represented the dead Body of Christ, stained and besprinkled with His Precious Blood, taken down from the Cross and laid in the arms of the Blessed Virgin, which, as a sanctified paten, received the Body of her well-beloved Son. The third, or smallest particle, is immersed in the Chalice, and this is said to represent the descent of the separated Soul of Christ into Limbo.

A Threefold Peace

BUT before this small particle is lowered into the Chalice, three Crosses are made with it over the Chalice, while the priest says, "*Pax Domini sit semper vobiscum* — The peace of the Lord be always with you," to signify that through the Passion and Death of Christ three testaments of peace were established and confirmed, or that the peace of God was confirmed in three classes of persons: First, there was confirmed the peace of eternal beatitude, and this peace was announced as soon as the Soul of Christ descended into the Limbo of the Fathers to the souls therein detained, whom He afterwards glorified. The action reminds us of that eternal peace purchased by Christ which He has conferred and will confer upon all the just souls in His everlasting kingdom.

Secondly, peace is conferred through the same Passion and Death upon the just on earth by grace and the friendship of God; and thirdly, peace is given even to sinners, inasmuch as they are invited to repentance and pardon, and are offered the means of reconciliation with God.

Or again, it may be said of the three kinds of peace signified by the three Crosses that one is the peace of grace or union with God, the second, internal peace of heart with oneself and the third, fraternal peace with one's neighbor and with all men.

Mingling of the Species

THE mingling of the species after the breaking of the Sacred Host symbolizes the resurrection of Christ. Whilst in the previous separation the sacred species represent His bloody death, they afterwards, by their reunion, become the symbol of His glorious resurrection. In the prayer, "May this mingling and consecration of the Body and Blood of our Lord Jesus Christ be to us who receive It effectual unto eternal life," the word consecration is not used in the sense of a translation to a more elevated or a more holy state, or of greater sanctification, for Christ's Body and Blood cannot be further sanctified. This word may also signify the dedication and gift of a person or an object to God. In this latter sense it is used here, for in the act of mingling, Christ appears as the resuscitated, living Pasch, and as such is presented or offered to God.

This mixture or mingling of the Body and Blood of Christ, which is made under the sacramental species, seems to signify that although in the Consecration the separation of Body and Blood which occurred in His Passion and Death is symbolized, now, however, in heaven, His glorious Body is not separated from His Blood; and, in like manner, in this Sacrament the Body of Christ is not really separated from His Blood, but united to It, although mystically they are represented by the sacramental species as separated.

The Divine Lamb of Sacrifice

Agnus Dei

WHEN St. John the Baptist, on the banks of the Jordan, beheld our Savior approaching, he exclaimed: "Behold the Lamb of God! —Behold Him who taketh away the sins of the world." These words are now addressed to our Savior in the Mass.

The celebrant, standing, with hands joined, and head inclined, towards the Sacred-Host, says aloud:

Agnus Dei, qui tollis peccata mundi.	Lamb of God, who takest away the sins of the world.

Having said these words, he rests his left hand on the corporal, and, striking his breast with his right hand as a sign of contrition, he continues:

Miserere nobis.	Have mercy on us.

This he does a second and a third time, but the third time, instead of saying "Miserere nobis," he concludes with the words, "Dona nobis pacem—Grant us peace."

It is generally acknowledged that this prayer was introduced into the Mass by Pope St. Sergius I in the latter part of the seventh century. At first it concluded each time with the petition, *Miserere nobis*, but later on (some time in the thirteenth century) the invocation *Dona nobis pacem* was substituted after the third recital of the *Agnus Dei*, as a prayer for peace in the many calamities and disturbances that had befallen the Church at that time.

In Requiem Masses the petition of the Agnus Dei is differently rendered, inasmuch as we twice implore of the Divine Sacrificial Lamb rest for the suffering souls from their pains and sorrows, and the third time we implore for them eternal rest in heaven: *Dona eis requiem,* — *Dona eis requiem sempiternam.*

In the Old Testament the lamb was one of the victims most commonly sacrificed to God, and was therefore a special type of the Savior. The Paschal lamb was in an especial manner a type of Christ, the true Lamb, who was to take away the sins of the world by atoning for them by His Blood. Christ's death was to fulfill what was merely indicated by the death of the sacrificial lamb in the Temple, namely, atonement for and remission of the sins of the world. It was, therefore, but natural that John the Baptist should present the Savior under that figure.

The prayers of the Mass thus far are almost all addressed to God the Father, but now the *Agnus Dei* and the three following prayers are addressed to God the Son, made man for us. This formula of prayer, taken in part from Holy Scripture (John 1: 29), has a wealth and depth of meaning. In the first place, it discloses the sublimity of the Divine sacrificial Lamb given by God and again offered to Him, who innocently, meekly and freely underwent the death of the Cross. In the next place, it exalts the sin-effacing, world-redeeming power and efficacy of His sacrificial death. And finally, it contains a humble, sorrowful, contrite appeal for mercy and for the obtaining of peace.

In the *Agnus Dei* we implore our Lord Jesus Christ, who is present before us in the Blessed Sacrament, to have mercy on us, acknowledging at the same time our weakness, our sins and our many defects, as well as those of which we may have been guilty during the Holy Sacrifice by distraction, tepidity or irreverence. We furthermore beg our Savior to forgive all our sins, and to supply for our imperfections and negligences by offering Himself for us to His Heavenly Father.

Three times we strike our breasts at this prayer, because we desire to be forgiven for three kinds of sins—sins of thought, word and deed. Again, we repeat the Agnus Dei three times, that Christ may take away from us three species of sins, namely, of weakness, of ignorance and of malice.

The Sacrificial Lamb on our altar has become a sacrifice to the infinite love of God and a sacrifice to the dreadful malice of sin. The love of God sent Him upon earth to man; the hatred of man has slain Him. Thus in Jesus love and sin have met. The mighty drama of Divine love battling with sin was performed on Calvary in a visible manner; invisibly it is repeated daily and hourly in Holy Mass. The Divine Lamb on the altar is the same as the Divine Lamb on Golgotha, and His love and merits have the same value before the Eternal Father as at that time. Here His Sacred Heart glows with the same fire of love for God and men that inspired It upon the Cross, and consecrates Itself to the Father as a sacrifice of praise, of thanksgiving, of atonement and of petition.

In the past we have often and grievously offended God, despised His commandments and returned ingratitude for His benefits. Jesus is our Sacrifice—He has been slain for the atonement of our sins. Let us turn to Him now with loving and grateful hearts. He is the pure Lamb, the holy Lamb, the innocent Lamb, who was immolated for us, and whose Blood has redeemed us from our sins. Let us, therefore, say these three invocations with great fervor, imploring Him to cleanse our souls from all stain, that they may be pure for the reception of His Sacred Body and Blood in Holy Communion. Let us offer the Sacrificial Lamb to God the Father as a recompense for all the benefits He has bestowed upon us, and as an atonement for all the evil we have committed. Let us offer the Immaculate Lamb now immolated upon the altar, that by His superabundant merits we may acquire the graces necessary to live a holy life and to die a holy and happy death.

The Three Prayers after the Agnus Dei

THE prayers after the *Agnus Dei* and before the Communion were not inserted in the Missal by any ancient pontifical institution or composition, but were evidently composed and handed down through tradition by holy and religious men. Their insertion seems to have taken place sometime between the eleventh and thirteenth centuries. These prayers were originally private, and intended especially for the priest: for this reason they have this peculiarity, that the petitions are in the singular number, referring to the celebrant only. However, as in the prayers of the Mass the priest prays not only for himself, but for all the faithful, so these prayers, too, express the petitions and the needs of each individual assisting at the adorable Sacrifice and uniting with the priest in offering it.

The celebrant inclines, joins his hands with the tips of the little fingers touching the front edge of the altar, his eyes fixed upon the Sacred Host, and repeats the three prayers in succession. The first of these is a prayer for peace:

Domine Jesu Christe, qui dixisti Apostolis tuis: Pacem relinquo vobis, pacem meam do vobis: ne respicias peccata mea, sed fidem Ecclesiae; tuae: eamque secundum voluntatem tuam pacificare et coadunare digneris. Qui vivis et regnas Deus, per omnia saecula saeculorum. Amen.	[14]O Lord Jesus Christ, who didst say to Thy Apostles, peace I leave with you, My peace I give unto you; regard not my sins, but the faith of Thy Church, and vouchsafe to her that peace and unity which is agreeable to Thy will. Who livest and reignest, God forever and ever. Amen.

Still pervaded with longing for peace which he has just implored of the Lamb of God, the priest now begs this happiness for the Holy Catholic Church—for the Church, through which and for which he stands at the altar; for the Church, which is so furiously attacked and persecuted by the world and therefore expects fidelity and readiness for sacrifice from her priests; for the Church, which has adorned him with the stole of the priesthood, . . . has given him a wonderful, supernatural power, . . . has entrusted to him the keys of heaven; for the Church, his pride, his love, his Mother. And what a mother! She is the queen who wears the diadem of precious virtues, the crown of sanctity. Is it not natural that his fervent prayer is in the first place for this Mother?

In order to give to this petition the proper emphasis and to guarantee its being granted, he appeals to the last will and testament of Jesus, as it were, reminding Him of His promise to His Apostles:

"Peace I leave with you; My peace I give to you" (John 14: 27). And indeed, what peace do we not derive from the consciousness that God is our loving Father who directs everything for our good and will never desert us in any necessity!

---

[13] *This prayer is omitted in Masses for the departed.*

In order that his sins and ours may not hinder the granting of this petition, the priest again has recourse to the Communion of Saints, but in this instance he appeals, not to the saints in heaven, but rather to the holy souls who are still in the bosom of the Church Militant. He begs God not to regard our sins, but to look with complacency upon the living faith and the good works which adorn the lives of so many deserving children of the Church. In uttering these words with the priest we should entertain the humble conviction that all who are assisting at Holy Mass are far worthier and better before God than we are, and that we must unite ourselves with their faith and purity in order to gain God's favor.

In Solemn High Mass, the *Pax* or *kiss of peace* is here given, to signify that we should not approach Holy Communion without having forgiven those who may have offended us.

The other two prayers serve as an immediate preparation for Holy Communion. Notwithstanding their simplicity, these two prayers are highly inspirational and contain the very best that we can say to Our Lord before receiving Holy Communion: —

Domine Jesu Christe, Fili Dei vivi qui ex voluntate Patris, cooperante Spiritu Sancto, per mortem tuam mundum vivificasti: libera me per hoc sacrosanctum Corpus et Sanguinem tuum, ab omnibus iniquitatibus meis, et universis malis, et fac me tuis semper inhaerere mandatis, et a te numquam separari permittas. Qui cum eodem Deo Patre et Spiritu Sancto vivis et regnas Deus in saecula saeculorum. Amen.	O Lord Jesus Christ, Son of the living God, who according to the will of the Father, through the cooperation of the Holy Ghost, hast by Thy death given life to the world: deliver me by this, Thy most sacred Body and Blood, from all my iniquities and from all evils; and make me always adhere to Thy commandments, and never suffer me to be separated from Thee. Who with the same God the Father and the Holy Ghost, livest and reignest, God, forever and ever. Amen.

The Divine Lamb of Sacrifice

Perceptio Corporis tui, Domine Jesu Christe, quod ego indignus sumere praesumo, non mihi proveniat in judicium et condemnationem: sed pro tua pietate prosit mihi ad tutamentum mentis et corporis, et ad medelam percipiendam. Qui vivis et regnas cum Deo Patre in unitate Spiritus Sancti Deus, per omnia saecula saeculorum. Amen

Let not the participation of Thy Body, O Lord Jesus Christ, which I, unworthy, presume to receive, turn to my judgment and condemnation; but through Thy goodness may it be to me a safeguard and remedy both of soul and body. Who with God the Father in the unity of the Holy Ghost, livest and reignest, God, forever and ever. Amen.

Very appropriately do we here address Our Lord with the words of St. Peter: "O Lord Jesus Christ, Son of the Living God." Peter saw but the humanity of Christ, yet he professed His Divinity, and for that reason was called blessed. On the altar we see neither the humanity nor the Divinity of Christ, yet we profess both with a firm faith. May we not hope, then, that this profession will win for us the same reward of praise as that which Our Lord bestowed upon His Apostle?

Mention is made of the obedience with which Christ submitted to the will of His Heavenly Father and yielded to death in order to restore life to a fallen race. We implore Our Lord to vouchsafe to apply to us the blessing of His bloody Sacrifice, first, by forgiving us all our sins and their temporal punishment, and preserving us from all evil; and secondly, by giving us the grace of inviolable fidelity and indissoluble union with Him. The petition for this latter favor is particularly affecting: *Never permit me to be separated from Thee.* We have need of Jesus at every moment, at every step we take; without Him we can do nothing. We ought, therefore, often to acknowledge our dependence upon Him and confidently implore His assistance. This petition is likewise an ardent appeal for the grace of final perseverance which is an added motive for our saying it with attention and devotion.

In the third prayer we ask that the reception of the Sacred Body of Christ may not turn to our judgment and condemnation, but may protect and save us in body and soul. Holy Communion makes us spiritually and corporally one with Jesus—His Blood relation, as it were. Yet, if we were to receive Him unworthily, this holy Sacrament would, on the contrary, separate us from Him and become for us a source of eternal damnation. This thought fills us with anxiety and we implore our Savior, through His loving kindness, to preserve us from such a grievous misfortune.

The Eucharistic Banquet

The Priest's Communion

FOR the completion of a sacrifice, communion with the victim is necessary. In the unbloody Sacrifice of the Lord, this takes place at Holy Communion, wherein Christ becomes the food of the faithful. By means of this food and through this food, the faithful enjoy communion with the Divinity. And as it is the priest through whom Christ offers this sacrifice, the priest's Communion suffices for the consummation of the sacrifice, though Holy Church is desirous that the faithful also should receive the Body and Blood of Christ as often as they assist at Holy Mass. According to the very idea of this sacrifice, and of other sacrifices typical of it, both under the natural law and the Mosaic law, the celebrating priest should partake of the Sacrificial Victim. So stringent is the law of the Church in this matter that it ordains, in case of the celebrant's becoming ill or otherwise unable to complete the Mass after the Con-

The Eucharistic Banquet

secration, that another priest, even though he be not tasting, should be required to do so. In order that the Communion may be received and that an integral part of the Mass may not be omitted.

Having said the three foregoing prayers, the celebrant rests his hands on the corporal and genuflects. Then with the forefinger of his right hand he reverently moves the two parts of the Sacred Host toward the edge of the paten, and, placing them together in their original round form, he puts them between the forefinger and thumb of the left hand, also placing the paten between the fingers of the same hand, while he prays:

Panem coelestem accipiam, et nomen Domini invocabo.	I will take the Bread of heaven, and call upon the Name of the Lord.

The last words are taken from Psalm 115: 4, and must have been introduced into the Mass at a very early date, since St. Augustine (430 A. D.) comments upon them, saying that they are an expression of ardent desire. To call upon or invoke God is to invite Him to come to us, to be our strength, our light and our life. To invoke God means also to adore and thank Him—to render Him, in a word, all the duties of religion.

Supporting the paten and the Sacred Host, in this manner with his left hand, raised a little above the corporal, and inclining slightly, the priest says three times in a modulated voice, striking his breast each time with the three fingers of his right hand:

Domine, non sum dignus, ut intres sub tectum meum: sed tantum dic verbo, et sanabitur anima mea.	Lord, I am not worthy that Thou shouldst enter under my roof; say but the word, and my soul shall be healed.

Only the words: "Domine, non sum dignus," are to be said audibly.

The priest, like the centurion of old, realizes his utter unworthiness to receive so great a grace as a visit from our Savior. Yet, secure in the hope that his faith will be rewarded as was that of the centurion, he repeats these words with humility, faith, and confidence, and we should repeat them with him in the same sentiments.

Standing erect, the priest now takes into his right hand the two parts of the Sacred Host, makes with them the Sign of the Cross before him over the paten, and with bowed head says the words:

Corpus Domini nostri Jesu Christi custodiat animam meam in vitam aeternam. Amen.	May the Body of our Lord Jesus Christ preserve my soul unto life everlasting. Amen.

Then, placing the two parts of the Sacred Host over each other, inclining moderately, and resting his forearms upon the altar, the priest receives both parts of the Sacred Host.

Thus Jesus enters the heart of His servant and representative, there to work wonders of grace and mercy as He did in the house of the centurion. The Divine Lamb makes Himself the food of His priest and people: *Factus cibus viatorum!*

After receiving the Sacred Host, the celebrant places the paten on the corporal at the foot of the chalice toward the Gospel side of the altar. Standing erect, he purifies his fingers over the paten, and joining his hands near his face, with his head slightly inclined, he remains a few moments in meditation.

Having finished the short meditation after the reception of the Sacred Host, the celebrant separates his hands, uncovers the chalice, genuflects in the usual manner, and then with the left hand he holds the paten inclined over the chalice and with the index finger of the right hand wipes off any particles found on the paten. Then with the paten he collects any small particles which may be upon the corporal, saying at the same time:

Quid retribuam Domino pro omnibus, quae retribuit mihi? Calicem salutaris accipiam, et nomen Domini invocabo. Laudans invocabo Dominum, et ab inimicis meis salvus ero.	What shall I render to the Lord for all He hath rendered unto me? I will take the Chalice of Salvation, and call upon the Name of the Lord. Praising, I will call upon the Lord, and I shall be saved from my enemies

Holding the paten with his left hand, the priest cleanses it with the forefinger and thumb of the right hand so that any particles adhering to it may fall into the chalice. After purifying his fingers, he rests his left hand, still holding the paten, on the altar, and taking the chalice in his right hand, he says the words: "Calicem salutaris accipiam... — I will take the Chalice of Salvation, and call upon the Name of the Lord. Praising, I will call upon the Lord, and I shall be saved from my enemies."

THE EUCHARISTIC BANQUET

Holy Church places these words upon the lips of the priest in answer to his earnest inquiry by what means he may make an adequate return for the unspeakable Gift which God has just bestowed upon him. Ah! the Chalice of Salvation—the Chalice of the Precious Blood of Jesus! A second time he will receive Our Lord, this time under a different form, and this Communion will be his thanksgiving for the first! A greater gift than this even God cannot bestow, for there is nothing more precious in heaven or on earth than the Body and Blood of Jesus. For us, too, there is no better means of thanksgiving for Holy Communion than to approach the Holy Table again as soon as possible, thereby to prove our appreciation and our gratitude to God for having given us His beloved Son to be the food of our souls.

After the priest has finished this prayer, he raises the chalice over the paten, which is held under it by the left hand, and makes the Sign of the Cross with it, whilst he says the words:—

Sanguis Domini nostri Jesu Christi custodiat animam meam in vitam aeternam. Amen.

May the Blood of our Lord Jesus Christ preserve my soul unto life everlasting. Amen.

Then, raising the paten under his chin, he reverently receives the Precious Blood, not removing the chalice from his lips until he has drained it.

The sacrifice is consummated. The Savior's mission as the Lamb of Sacrifice is fulfilled. He is no longer on the altar. . . The sacramental forms have been consumed. . . they have vanished from sight.

COMMUNION OF THE FAITHFUL

ALREADY in apostolic times it was customary to administer Holy Communion to the faithful during Holy Mass; in fact, in the early ages it was not administered outside of the Mass except to the sick or to those in prison or otherwise prevented from attending Holy Mass. For the first twelve centuries, it was customary for the faithful to receive under both species (when receiving during Holy Mass), but for wise and sufficient reasons the Church in time withdrew the Chalice from the use of the laity, exercising in this the power granted her by her Divine Founder of regulating the manner of the reception of the sacraments.

Since the days of Blessed Pius X, the practice of frequent and daily Holy Communion is becoming ever more widespread. The faithful realize more and more that in this Sacrament alone they can find strength to resist the storms of temptation of our evil days arid to preserve the Faith in its vigor and purity. At Holy Mass, therefore, it is a most consoling and edifying sight to see numbers of the faithful approach the Holy Table, that with the priest they may receive more abundantly the fruits of the Sacrifice.

After the celebrant has received the Precious Blood, the acolyte, kneeling at the Epistle side of the altar, repeats the *Confiteor* as a public declaration of sorrow for sin on the part of those who are about to receive the Blessed Eucharist. The communicants should join in saying this prayer with sentiments of humility and contrition. The *Confiteor* is designed to awaken in us the rueful acknowledgment of our own most grievous fault, and at the same time to move us to look up confidently to the Blessed Mother of God and to those pure souls who with us form the Communion of Saints and are our intercessors with God.

The priest then turns toward the people (without turning his back to the Blessed Sacrament), and says: —

Misereatur vestri omnipotens Deus et, dimissis peccatis vestris, perducat vos ad vitam aeternam. ℟. Amen	May almighty God have mercy upon you, forgive you your sins and bring you to life everlasting. ℟. Amen.

Making the Sign of the Cross over the people, he pronounces the absolution: —

The Eucharistic Banquet

Indulgentiam, absolutionem, et remissionem peccatorum vestrorum, tribuat vobis omnipotens et misericors Dominus. ℟. *Amen.*	May the almighty and merciful Lord grant you pardon, absolution, and remission of your sins. ℟. Amen.

The *Misereatur* and *Indulgentiam* are the reply of the Church to the supplication contained in the *Confiteor*, and implore for us the Divine mercy and the remission of the sins of which we have repented.

Now the celebrant, having turned, toward the altar and genuflected, turns once more toward the congregation and holds aloft one of the small Hosts with the thumb and forefinger of his right hand, while he again repeats the words of the Precursor: —

Ecce Agnus Dei, ecce qui tollit pecata mundi.	Behold the Lamb of God, behold Him who taketh away the sins of the world.

He then adds immediately:

Domine, non sum dignus, ut intres sub tectum meum: sed tantum dic verbo, et sanabitur anima mea.	Lord, I am not worthy that Thou shouldst enter under my roof; say but the word, and my soul shall be healed.

This last sentence he repeats three times, the communicants uniting with him and striking their breasts at each repetition, in attestation of their sorrow for ever having sinned and of their unworthiness to receive the Body and Blood of their Redeemer. The words of this prayer express the best disposition for Holy Communion—namely, humility and an acknowledgment of our imperfection and misery. They also express our confidence in our Divine Savior, that He will take away any stains of sin which may be obstacles to the fruits of a good, worthy Communion.

The priest then descends to the Communion rail and administers Holy Communion. Holding one of the consecrated Hosts in his right hand, he makes

the Sign of the Cross with It, to signify that this is the very Body of Jesus Christ which hung upon the Cross, and then places the Sacred Host on the tongue of the communicant with the words:

Corpus Domini nostri Jesu Christi custodiat animam tuam in vitam aeternam. Amen.

May the Body of our Lord Jesus Christ preserve thy soul unto life everlasting. Amen.

Holding the paten under their chin, with their eyes reverently lowered, the head moderately raised, the mouth conveniently opened, and the tip of the tongue resting upon the lower lip, the communicants successively receive the Body of Christ. After receiving the Sacrament, they should incline for a moment in silent adoration and then retire from the railing, not with a hasty, but with a decorus step, with downcast eyes and becoming gravity.

Heavenly graces are promised to those who partake of this most sacred Banquet of the Body and Blood of Christ. How we must admire the dispensations of Providence in giving us this precious Food of our souls under the form of bread! "What is sweeter, more precious and more blissful than this Divine Food?" exclaims St. Thomas of Villanova. "The hungry person partakes thereof and is satiated; the needy receives It and has his fill; the depressed partakes of It, and is inebriated with heavenly bliss; the just partakes of It and becomes still more just; the devout penitent partakes of It and becomes purified; the infirm partakes of It and receives the grace of spiritual convalescence; the dying person, partakes of It and takes with him the surest pledge of eternal life!" Truly, It is the pledge of every heavenly blessing and grace!

Mutual Longing Satisfied

THE moments which immediately follow Holy Communion are most precious and rich in graces. We have hospitably received Our Lord into the abode of our heart; we have satisfied not only our longing to receive Him, but also His longing to be united with us. There is no more fitting or efficacious time to thank God for His favors and to implore new ones than in the precious moments after Holy Communion, when Our Lord Himself, with Body and Soul, Divinity and Humanity reposes in our breast. It is then the floodgates of His mercy are open to us, and if through our own negligence we fail to draw from His fountains of salvation, we have only ourselves to blame for the lack of profit we derive from this most inestimable Sacrament.

It is but natural, then, that we should remain a reasonable time in thanksgiving and adoration, at least until the Species are consumed, which is generally conceded to be about the space of ten or fifteen minutes. Surely a quarter of an hour is not too much for one's thanksgiving; it is indeed but very little. Considering that some of the saints spent hours in loving converse with Our Lord after Holy Communion, we may realize how unbecoming it is to leave the Church after only a few minutes' thanksgiving. St. Philip Neri once saw a person turning his steps toward the church door very soon after having received Holy Communion, evidently with the intention of leaving. The saint immediately ordered two choir boys to accompany him with lighted candles. The man, astounded at this action, inquired of St. Philip what was the purpose of this ceremony, and the latter answered with grave courtesy: "When a priest carries the Blessed Sacrament in a ciborium he is invariably accompanied by two boys with lighted candles, and it seems to me that a similar honor ought to be paid to him who bears the Holy Eucharist in his heart." Thereupon, the man, greatly ashamed, knelt down to offer Jesus the acts of adoration and thanksgiving which were His due.

The supreme and all-embracing object of the Sacrifice receives its fullest expression in the Communion of the priest and the people. The sacrificial action terminates with a sacrificial feast, in which the Victim is taken as food. At this sacred Banquet the adopted sons of God sit down with the natural Son, who made them heirs to His kingdom; they appropriate the benefits of His Passion and receive a tangible pledge and a foretaste of the glory that awaits them. At the Eucharistic Banquet we may represent our Savior sitting in the midst as our Father, the Church as our Mother, and all the faithful as children, who attend with sweet confidence to partake of the Bread of Life.

"Oh, how sweet, Lord, is Thy spirit," the Church prays in the Office of Corpus Christi, "who, that Thou mightest show Thy sweetness to the sons of men, feedest them with the most delightful bread from heaven, fillest the hungry with good things, and sendest the disdainful rich away empty."

Holy Church never tires of inviting us, never ceases to urge us to receive Holy Communion frequently, yes, daily; and she encourages us, whenever we assist at the holy Sacrifice of the Mass, to receive the Blessed Sacrament with the priest, not only spiritually, by way of desire, but actually by the sacramental participation of the Sacred Species. This is but the expression of the desires of her Divine Spouse, who has entrusted to her this precious Treasure for the welfare of her children.

The Divine Heart of Jesus burns with desire to communicate Itself to those who assist at the Holy Sacrifice. "Take and eat," He says: "this is My Body" (Matt. 26: 26). Ah! how that loving Heart is grieved when the priest places consecrated Hosts again into the tabernacle, which could have been placed in living tabernacles of the hearts of pious Christians had they communicated. The Little Flower of Jesus says so touchingly: "Jesus does not come down from heaven each morning in order to remain in a golden ciborium, but to find another heaven—the heaven of our souls, in which He takes His delight." Could we but realize the vehement, desire of Jesus to be received by us in Holy Communion, we would not absent ourselves from the Holy Table without grave reasons. Altar, tabernacle, monstrance, church, are for His love only transient abodes: His aim is directed toward our hearts. It is there He longs to repose. He begs, He pleads. He conjures us to open to Him our hearts. He makes most glorious promises to those who receive Him; He threatens with eternal death those who refuse to partake of His Body and Blood.

Wonderful are the effects which Holy Communion produces in the soul of the worthy communicant. It unites the soul with Jesus Christ the Author of life. It is the pledge of eternal glory and the fountain of all spiritual graces. It restores health to the soul, and oftentimes imparts health and strength even to the body. It effaces venial sin and conquers the power of Satan. It rejoices the soul with heavenly bliss. Did we but realize how many treasures we lose for ourselves and for others when we remain away from Holy Communion, we should hasten frequently, yes, daily, to this fountain of grace and Divine mercy, to this source of all good and holiness.

The Ablution Prayers

ACCORDING to the teaching of our holy faith, Jesus Christ, whole and entire, is present under the smallest particle of the sacramental Species, and hence the Church has prescribed minute rubrics for the purification of the celebrant's fingers and the chalice after the Communion, so as to prevent any irreverence or profanation of the Blessed Sacrament.

The celebrant, after having replaced the ciborium in the tabernacle (standing at the center of the altar, his left hand resting in the middle of the corporal and holding the paten between his fingers) with his right hand offers the chalice to the acolyte toward the Epistle side to receive the wine of ablution. At the same time he prays:

Quod ore sumpsimus, Domine, pura mente capiamus; et de munere temporali fiat nobis remedium sempiternum.	Grant, O Lord, that what we have taken with our mouth we may receive with a pure mind; and that from a temporal gift it may become for us an eternal remedy.

The acolyte pours into the chalice about the same quantity of wine as was used for the Consecration. The priest turns the chalice around, so that the wine may circulate on the sides and cover the whole space touched by the consecrated Species; then He receives the so-called "first ablution," holding the paten underneath his chin as he drinks from the chalice.

This prayer is very ancient and contains two petitions: first, that the outward administration of sacramental Communion may produce many graces in us by the reception of the Heavenly Guest into a heart purified from all attachment to earthly and transient things and filled with love and longing for the treasures of eternity; and secondly, that Holy Communion may guide us unto eternal life.

By this prayer a distinction is made between communion of the tongue and communion of the soul, because some, unfortunately, who receive the Body of the Lord, are not spiritually nourished by Him. They communicate with His Body, but not, or only little, with His Spirit and affections. To these—yea, to all who approach the Holy Table — may well be addressed the warning of St. Paul to the Corinthians: "Brethren, I exhort you that you receive not the grace of God in vain." Just as a sick man who received medicine into his hands, but did not take it internally, would indeed have received the medicine but in a useless and fruitless way, so too, we receive the grace of God in vain when we receive it at the gate of our heart and not within the inmost of our soul. It is only by partaking of the Spirit of Christ, His truth, His holiness—in a word, by intercommunion of souls— that the heavenly gifts bestowed Upon us in time will heal our souls of all evil in this life and avail us unto life everlasting.

Communion is here termed a "temporal gift," partly because the Sacrifice and the Sacrament are intended only for the time of our earthly pilgrimage and partly because they are consummated in a short time. But though the sacramental presence lasts only a few minutes, if we consider the end for which Our Lord gave us His Flesh as food and His Blood as drink, and the effects which they produce, we must conclude that the union of Christ's Flesh with our flesh has its completion only in the union of the spirit, which, if not interrupted by sin, will continue during our whole life and throughout eternity.

After drinking the wine of purification, the priest places the paten on the rear part of the corporal and the chalice on the fore part, in front of the paten, then, holding his forefingers and thumb over the cup of the chalice which he supports with the other fingers he goes to the Epistle side where the acolyte pours first wine and then water over his fingers into the chalice. Meanwhile the celebrant prays:

Corpus tuum, Domine, quod sumpsi, et Sanguis quem potavi, adhaereat visceribus meis; et praesta; ut in me non remaneat scelerum macula, quem pura et sancta refecerunt sacramenta. Qui vivis et regnas in saecula saeculorum Amen.	May Thy Body, O Lord, which I have received, and Thy Blood which I have drunk, cleave to my bowels; and grant that no stain of sin may remain in me, whom Thy pure and holy sacraments have refreshed; who livest and reignest world without end. Amen.

Having received the wine and water into the chalice, the priest extends it toward the corporal and places it on the altar, without withdrawing his fingers. With his right hand he then takes the purificator and dries his fingers while going to the middle of the altar. While consuming the ablution, he holds the purificator, folded over the left forefinger, under his chin. He then places the chalice in the center of the corporal and wipes his fingers, his lips, and the interior of the chalice, with the purificator. After this he covers the chalice toward the Gospel side, placing over it the purificator, the paten, the pall, the veil and the burse containing the folded corporal used at Mass.

As this latter prayer is in the singular and presupposes that Holy Communion has been received under both forms, it appears to be intended and destined for the celebrant alone, whilst the preceding prayer may be applicable to all who have received Communion. The priest prays that the transient sacramental presence of the Savior may produce interior and permanent effects and that it may adhere to his innermost soul, not as to substance but as to virtue and efficacy, by removing all stains of sin and preserving from them in the future.

Communion Antiphon

While the priest is drying and covering the chalice, the acolyte removes the Missal to the Epistle side of the altar. The priest, with hands joined, then reads aloud from the Missal a short antiphon called the "Communion."

THE Communion antiphon does not necessarily refer to the reception of the Holy Eucharist, as might be supposed by its name and position. In former times it took the form of a canticle and was sung while the people were receiving Holy Communion, from whence it derives its name. It refers to the particular Sunday or feast which is being celebrated, or to the purpose for which the Mass is being offered, and like the Introit, Gradual, and Offertory, varies with each Mass. The Communion for Corpus Christi reads:

Quotiescumque manducabitis panem hunc, et calicem bibetis, mortem Domini annuntiabitis, donec veniat: itaque quicumque manducaverit panem, biberit calicem Domini indigne, reus erit Corporis et Sanguinis Domini. Alleluia.	As often as you shall eat this bread, and drink the chalice, you shall show forth the death of the Lord, until He come: therefore whosoever shall eat this bread or drink the chalice of the Lord unworthily, shall be guilty of the Body and Blood of the Lord. Alleluia.

In this instance the *Communion* does refer to the reception of the Holy Eucharist, because that is the central theme

The Eucharistic Banquet

of the feast of Corpus Christi. It is as if the Church, by repeating the solemn words of the Epistle, would remind us again of the necessity of purifying our hearts before venturing to approach the sacred banquet of the most pure Body and Blood of Christ. She praises, as it were, those who have received Holy Communion worthily, and issues a solemn warning to such as may have dared to approach the Holy Table in the state of mortal sin.

In High Mass the Communion antiphon is sung by the choir. It is an expression of joy and gladness, and in a mystical sense signifies the resurrection of Christ, over which heaven and earth rejoice and the multitude of angels exult.

Postcommunion

After the Communion antiphon the priest returns to the center, kisses the altar, and turning to the people, greets them with the words "Dominus vobiscum" to which the acolyte gives the usual response, "Et cum spiritu tuo." He then goes again to the Epistle side of the altar and with extended hands reads the prayer (or prayers) known as the "Postcommunion."'''

THE *Postcommunion* is similar in form to the *Collect* and the *Secret*. Like them, it varies according to the Sunday or festival. It is introduced by the word *Oremus*, an invitation to the faithful to join in prayer with the priest, and ends with the usual form, *Per omnia saecula saeculorum*. Other Postcommunion prayers may be added, to correspond with the additional *Collects* and *Secret* prayers.

In the *Postcommunion* prayers the priest and people return thanks for their participation in the Eucharistic Sacrifice, and pray God to preserve in them the abundant fruits of this sublime oblation of this celestial food. Each sacrament has its special fruit for those who receive it; The special fruit of the Holy Eucharist is love and the strength to avoid sin. The *Postcommunion* for the feast of Corpus Christi is as follows:

Fac nos, quaesumus, Domine, Divinitatis tuae sempiterna fruitione repleri: quam pretiosi Corporis et Sanguinis tui temporalis perceptio praefigurat. Qui vivis...	Grant us, O Lord, we beseech Thee, that we may have to the full that eternal enjoyment of Thy Godhead, which is prefigured by Thy Precious Body and Blood which we receive in this present life. Who livest...

Conclusion of the Mass

THE solemn conclusion of the liturgical celebration would seem to be an admonition from our holy Mother the Church that we should go forth from the Mass, not with the feeling that something is ended, but rather that something is begun: that the Divine influence of the Mass may radiate into our daily lives, into our homes and into our activities. The liturgical prayers recited by the priest after the Communion are surprisingly brief. One might almost expect a longer period of thanksgiving to follow. But Holy Church apparently wishes to impress upon us that our entire day should be spent in sentiments of gratitude to God for the benefits He has bestowed upon us in Holy Mass and Communion. She wishes us to live in the spirit of the Mass throughout the day, and to show by our conduct that God's graces are bearing fruit in our lives. But at the same time she encourages all who can do so without neglecting their duty, to spend a reasonable time in church after the Mass is ended, to give thanks to God for His Divine benefits.

CONCLUSION OF THE MASS

"ITE, MISSA EST"

After the "Postcommunion," the priest closes the Missal, returns to the center, kisses the altar, and turning to the people, extends and then folds his hands, saying: "Dominus vobiscum," with the usual response. Then, still facing the people, the priest says: "Ite, missa est— Go, it is dismissed," announcing the conclusion of the Divine service and dismissing the faithful in a solemn manner.

OUR LORD Himself, by the lips of His minister, bids us depart, as He bade His disciples farewell before ascending into heaven. In a little while we shall leave the church; Our Lord sends us out again into the world, not that we may be submerged in its distractions, but that we, in His power, may announce the coming of the kingdom of God and bring peace to it. *"Say: Peace to this house! And if a son of peace be there, your peace shall rest upon him"* (Luke 10: 5, 6). But how can we bring peace and grace into the kingdom of God? St. Hippolyte, the martyr, tells us: "As soon as this Holy Sacrifice is ended, let everyone hasten to perform a good work."

Our soul is filled with a solemn splendor and radiant joy —Christ is within us! We have not only "seen" His glory, we carry it within us, "full of grace and truth." How differently we view life now! We look at it with the eyes of God. The duties of our state of life present themselves; we take them up with joy, for they have become resplendent and sanctified through the Sacrifice of Christ, in which we commended them. Sanctified to us is every day on which we assist at Holy Mass, with all the works of the day, labor and rest, success and failure.

To the salutation "Ite, missa est," the acolyte, in the name of the people, answers: "Deo gratias—Thanks be to God."

The faithful are mindful of the manifold blessings God has just conferred upon them. "There is nothing shorter and at the same time greater than this act of thanksgiving," says St. Augustine. This was formerly the end of the Mass, and the faithful were at liberty to leave. A few centuries ago the prayer to the Blessed Trinity was added.

Since the Middle ages, the *Ite missa est* has been regarded as a characteristic mark of the joyful days of the ecclesiastical year, and accordingly is employed only on the days when the *Gloria* is prayed. During the penitential seasons and on days when the *Gloria* is not said, the concluding formula is "*Benedicamus Domino* — Let us bless the Lord," to which the same response is made as above.

In Requiem Masses the concluding formula, is always "Requiescant in pace — May they rest in peace," with the response "Amen." The "Benedicamus Domino" and "Requiescant in pace" are said by the priest with face turned toward the altar.

"Deo Gratias"

THROUGHOUT the entire Mass there is a note of gratitude. Thanksgiving is the spirit we wish to preserve throughout the day as we possess it now at the conclusion of Holy Mass. Holy Mass gives us light, truth, grace; we should rejoice, and our joy should urge us to thank God for the immeasureable benefits which in His infinite goodness He so lavishly bestows upon us. But, poor and miserable as we are, how can we thank Him worthily? Ah, this good Lord has made it possible for us to fulfill the great duty of gratitude we owe Him. He has enabled us to render Him adequate thanks by offering to Him Jesus Christ in the holy Sacrifice of the Mass. In this manner we return to God perfect gratitude, we render perfect satisfaction, for in the Holy Sacrifice the priest offers Him a tribute of thanksgiving which corresponds to the greatness of His Divine gifts. A tribute worthy of God could not be offered by all the saints together, in their own power, but it can be done through Holy Mass.

Conclusion of the Mass

If from our earliest childhood up to the present hour we had continually thanked God upon our knees for all His gifts and graces, and if we had called upon all devout persons to join with us in our lifelong tribute of thanks, our thanksgiving would still fall short of the gratitude we owe to God. If, in addition, we invoked the glorious choirs of angels and saints to unite with us in our incessant praise and thanksgiving, the tribute of gratitude paid to God would still be infinitely less perfect than that rendered to Him by His Divine Son in *one single Holy Mass*. The reason for this is obvious; for the thanksgiving of all creatures in heaven and on earth is *finite*, whereas that of the Son of God, in virtue of His Divinity, is *infinite* in power and efficacy.

What a consoling truth! We, poor creatures, can give worthy thanks to God for His benefits. In Holy Mass Jesus is at our disposal; there we can offer Him to His Heavenly Father. St. Teresa, realizing the boundless graces God had bestowed on her, one day anxiously cried out: "My God, my God! what can I, a poor creature, do to thank Thee for the favors Thou hast lavished on me?" At the same moment she heard a voice from heaven saying distinctly: *Go to Mass!*

Let us take these words to heart for our own profit, and whenever we have had the happiness to assist at Holy Mass, thank God at its conclusion in some such words as these: "Praise and thanks be to Thee, O Lord Jesus Christ, from me and from all creatures, because out of Thy pure love Thou hast instituted Holy Mass and made it a channel of countless graces and mercies to us. As a fitting acknowledgement of Thy favors, I offer to Thee, and through Thee to the Holy Trinity, all the praise and thanksgiving rendered to Thee in all Holy Masses until the end of time. I beg the choirs of angels and all the company of the redeemed to praise and magnify Thee with us for all eternity."

The Treasures of the Mass

Prayer to the Holy Trinity

The celebrant, resting his hands, joined, upon the altar and moderately inclining, now prays:

Placeat tibi, sancta Trinitas, obsequium servitutis meae: et praesta; ut sacrificium, quod oculis tuae majestatis indignus obtuli, tibi sit acceptabile, mihique et omnibus pro quibus illud obtuli, sit, te miserante, propitiabile. Per Christum Dominum nostrum. Amen.

May the performance of my homage be pleasing to Thee, O Holy Trinity; and grant that the Sacrifice which I, though unworthy, have offered up in the sight of Thy Majesty, may be acceptable to Thee, and through Thy mercy be a propitiation for me and for all those for whom it has been offered. Through Christ our Lord. Amen.

THIS prayer, like so many prayers of the Mass, is an outburst of praise and thanksgiving. We have offered to God the sublime Sacrifice which delights heaven and earth. God has accepted with complacency this sublimest of oblations. The moment has come to end "the mystery of the great Sacrifice," and we bow down before the majesty and greatness of God for the last time to beg for mercy. We appeal to the Triune God, to almighty Power, to unsearchable Wisdom, to immeasurable Love. In the name and for the glorification of the Triune God the Holy Sacrifice was begun, continued and completed; to the Blessed Trinity it is now once more, and for the last time, recommended. Impressed with the consciousness of his frailty, sinfulness and unworthiness, the priest first implores that the Sacrifice offered up by him and the homage of profound submission thereby rendered may be graciously accepted and received by the Holy Trinity, and then begs that in virtue of the Divine pleasure taken in the Sacrifice, and of the Divine mercy, there may flow from the altar unto all for whom it was offered, reconciliation and grace.

CONCLUSION OF THE MASS

THE LAST BLESSING

AFTER concluding the prayer to the Blessed Trinity, the priest extends his hands upon the altar and kisses it. With what devotion he impresses this last kiss upon the altar stone, upon which has just rested the Blood of the Victim of Calvary for the praise and glory of the Triune God, for the benefit of Holy Church, for the perfection of the just, for the conversion of sinners and the relief of the suffering souls in purgatory! These graces overflow from the Blessed Trinity.

The priest, standing erect and raising his eyes to heaven, lifts his hands, joins them, inclines to the Crucifix and says:—

Benedicat vos omnipotens Deus;   May God almighty bless you;

Then, turning toward the people, he places his left hand on his breast, and makes the Sign of the Cross over them with the right hand whilst he says:

Pater, at Filius ✠ *et Spiritus Sanctus.*   Father, and Son ✠ and Holy Ghost.

The acolyte responds: "Amen."

Bishops and Prelates make a threefold Sign of the Cross in giving the blessing—first toward the left, then to the center, and lastly toward, the right—introducing the blessing with the versicles:

℣. *Sit nomen Domini benedictum.*   ℣. May the Name of the Lord be blessed.

℟. *Ex hoc nunc et usque in saeculum.*   ℟. From henceforth, now and forever.

℣. *Adjutorium nostrum in nomine Domini.*   ℣. Our help is in the Name of the Lord.

℟. *Qui fecit coelum et terram.*   ℟. Who made heaven and earth.

For the solemn blessing, the mitre is placed on the bishop's head and the crosier is held in his left hand.

In Requiem Masses the blessing is not given; those present, the living, are not then blessed, to indicate that all the sacrificial prayers and fruits are ordained to the benefit of the suffering souls in purgatory.

Blessing is in an especial manner the office of the priests of the Church. Even in the Old Law we frequently read that the priest stretched forth his hand to the people and blessed them. When the priest's hands are consecrated with holy oil, the ordaining bishop says this prayer: *"Vouchsafe, O Lord, to consecrate and sanctify these hands by this unction and our benediction, that whatever they shall bless may be blessed, and whatever they shall consecrate may be consecrated, in the Name of our Lord Jesus Christ."* And at the consecration of a bishop, the prelate says to the newly consecrated: *"Whatsoever thou shalt bless, may it be blessed, and whatsoever thou shalt sanctify may it be sanctified, and may the laying on of this consecrated hand be of service to all for salvation."*

The blessing of a priest or a bishop has, therefore, by virtue of his ordination, special and great efficacy, whenever it is imparted, and should be received with faith and reverence. The liturgical blessing, as such, can never be fruitless and inefficacious, provided that the recipient presents no obstacle. It is a petition of the Church, which is always heard and granted by God because it is supported by her authority and her sanctity, and is based on the infinite merits of Jesus Christ, on His Precious Blood and on His loving promises. Consequently, at the end of Holy Mass, the faithful should try to receive the final blessing piously and confidently, and at the same time direct their desire especially to that grace which each one requires on that particular day or for some particular need.

The blessing given at the end of the Sacrifice of the Mass is very powerful. The fullness of the blessing of the Triune God descends upon us; the blessing of the Father, to strengthen our weakness by His omnipotence; the blessing of the Son, to enlighten our blindness by His wisdom; the blessing of the Holy Spirit, to take away our malice by His goodness. Through this blessing the Spirit of God will animate us, the love of God enkindle us, the holiness of God sanctify us, the glory of God reign in us, the mercy of God encompass us, the beauty of God transport us, the sweetness of God permeate us and the peace of God take full possession of us. Received with proper dispositions, this blessing will be a shield against visible and invisible enemies during life and particularly at the hour of our death.

We should often during the day recall that we have assisted at Holy Mass in the morning. This will give a holy blessing to our work, to our life, during the day. It will keep us united with Christ. God's blessing will operate in all our thoughts and deeds. His blessing will support us in the weakness and misery of our fallen nature; His blessing will remind us again and again of the love which Jesus bears us. *Ite Missa est* ought to resound in our ears throughout the day, until another morning finds us again before the altar, hearing the same blessed words.

THE LAST GOSPEL

After the blessing, the priest goes to the Gospel side of the altar, and having for the last time greeted the people with the salutation "Dominus vobiscum," he makes the Sign of the Cross with his thumb first upon the altar card, or the missal if it is before him, then on his forehead, lips and breast, whilst he says:

Initium Sancti Evangelii secundum Joannem *(seu Sequentia* sancti Evangelii, etc.).	The *beginning* of the Holy Gospel according to St. John (or *Continuation* of the Holy Gospel, etc.).

The acolyte responds:

Gloria tibi, Domine.	Glory be to Thee, O Lord.

The priest continues:

In principio erat Verbum, et Verbum erat apud Deum, et Deus erat Verbum. Hoc erat in principio apud Deum. Omnia per ipsum facta sunt, et sine ipso factum est nihil quod factum est. In ipso vita erat, et vita erat lux hominum, et lux in tenebris lucet, et tenebrae eam non comprehenderunt. Fuit homo missus a Deo, cui nomen erat Joannes. Hic venit in testimonium, ut testimonium perhiberet de lumine, ut omnes crederent per illum. Non erat ille lux, sed ut testimonium perhiberet de lumine. Erat lux vera quae illuminat omnem hominem venientem in hunc mundum. In mundo erat, et mundus per ipsum factus est, et mundus eum non cognovit. In propria venit, et sui eum non receperunt; quotquot autem receperunt eum, dedit eis potestatem filios Dei fieri; his qui credunt in nomine ejus, qui non ex sanguinibus, neque ex voluntate carnis, neque ex voluntate viri, sed ex Deo nati sunt. (Hic genuflectitur.) ET VERBUM CARO FACTUM EST, *et habitavit in nobis: et vidimus gloriam ejus, gloriam quasi Unigeniti a Patre, plenum gratia: et veritatis.*

In the beginning was the Word, and the Word was with God, and the Word was God: the same was in the beginning with God. All things were made by Him, and without Him was made nothing that was made: in Him was life, and the life was the light of men; and the light shineth in darkness, and the darkness did not comprehend it. There was a man sent from God, whose name was John. This man came for a witness to give testimony of the light, that all men might believe through him. He was not the light, but was to give testimony of the light, that was the true light that enlighteneth every man that cometh into this world. He was in the world, and the world was made by Him, and the world knew Him not. He came unto His own, and His own received Him not. But as many as received Him, He gave them power to become the sons of God: to them that believe in His Name, who are born not of blood, nor of the will of the flesh, nor of the will of man, but of God. AND THE WORD WAS MADE FLESH *(here the people genuflect)*, and dwelt among us; and we saw His glory, the glory as it were of the Only-begotten of the Father, full of grace and truth.

USUALLY the last Gospel is the beginning of the Gospel of St. John as prescribed by Pope St. Pius V, but when a feast of high rank falls on a Sunday or on a feria (weekday) which has its own Gospel, the Gospel of the day is said at the end of the Mass instead of that of St. John. On certain vigils, also, if the Mass of the vigil is not celebrated, the Gospel proper to the vigil is said at the end.

The Gospel of St. John is very appropriate for the conclusion of the Mass, inasmuch as it sums up the principal mysteries of our Faith, namely, the creation of the world and the reparation for sin effected through the mystery of the incarnation. It signifies the desire of the Church to preach the Gospel throughout the whole world according to the command of our Divine Redeemer. It is a profession of faith in the Christian religion, and brings before the minds of priest and people Him who is offered in Sacrifice, and who is really, truly and substantially present in the Blessed Sacrament—His person. His Divine and human natures and His attributes.

At the words: "*Et Verbum caro factum est*—And the Word was made flesh," all genuflect in honor of the mystery of the incarnation. St. Gertrude was accustomed, at the repetition of these words, to bow her head in gratitude and say: *I thank and bless Thee, O good Jesus, that for love of me Thou didst deign to be made man.* Our Lord once appeared to her and revealed how pleasing to Him was this practice, and made this promise in behalf of all who should do likewise: *If anyone does this, I will graciously incline My head toward him in return, and will offer to God the Father all the fruit of My incarnation, with all the love of My Heart, for the increase of that man's blessedness and glory.*

At the end of the last Gospel the acolyte responds "*Deo gratias*—thanks be to God," as an expression of the gratitude of the faithful for the unspeakable graces which God has just bestowed upon them, and likewise as an invitation to those who have communicated, to continue for a while in their thanksgiving.

Deo gratias! Before the awful majesty of the adorable Trinity, how powerless we feel to offer worthy thanks. But let us with confidence turn once more to Jesus, the Victim of Sacrifice, our Mediator with the Father; and say to Him: "O Jesus, Thou knowest how utterly incapable I am of doing even the least thing without Thee. Therefore, as my thanksgiving I once more offer Thee, with Thy glorious Wounds, to the Most Blessed Trinity, to supply for all my deficiencies in the Divine service, particularly during this Holy Sacrifice. Oh, what confidence, what courage this thought gives me: Thou Thyself art my thanksgiving, Thou eternal Priest, eternal Victim, eternal Altar of God! Not a moment passes on earth in which the Blood from the Wound of Thy holy side does not flow in streams, to be received into the chalice of some one of Thy priests and offered to the honor and glory of the adorable Trinity."

Deo gratias! Thanks be to God for "His unspeakable gift," —the holy Sacrifice of the Mass, by which we offer to God the most sublime Sacrifice of praise and adoration, the noblest Sacrifice of thanksgiving, the most efficacious Sacrifice of atonement and the most powerful Sacrifice of petition, through Jesus Christ, in Jesus Christ, and with Jesus Christ.

Concluding Prayers

AFTER low Mass, the priest, kneeling at the foot of the altar, recites the prescribed prayers, i.e., three "Hail Marys," the "Salve Regina" (Hail, holy Queen), "O God, our refuge, etc." for the conversion of sinners, the prayer to St. Michael the Archangel for aid in the battle against the devil, and finally a triple invocation of the Sacred Heart of Jesus.

CONCLUSION OF THE MASS

These prayers (except the final invocation) were prescribed for the whole Church by Pope Leo XIII on the feast of the Epiphany, 1884, and an indulgence of 300 days granted for their recitation. Pope Pius X added the threefold invocation of the Sacred Heart, for which he granted an indulgence of 7 years when recited in public after Holy Mass. Pope Pius XI (May 30, 1934) increased the above indulgence of 300 days to 10 years, in addition to the Indulgence of 7 years granted for the invocation of the Sacred Heart. In the recitation of these prayers, the people respond to and join with the priest, as custom prescribes.

After the prayers are concluded, the priest rises, goes to the altar, takes the chalice in his hands, returns to the foot of the altar, genuflects and retires to the sacristy, preceded by the acolyte.

As a mark of respect, the faithful should remain standing or kneeling in their places until the priest has left the sanctuary. What a disedifying sight it is to see the people begin to crowd into the aisles and rush toward the door the moment the prayers are ended, as if eager to throw off the restraint of the Divine services. Rather ought they to show by their conduct that they are deeply penetrated with the spirit of the sublime Mysteries which they have just witnessed, and withdraw in a reverent and recollected manner from this holy place where the Divine Presence remains.

✠ ✠ ✠

REMARK: Here we wish to remark that private revelations, according to the decrees of Pope Urban VIII in the years 1634 and 1641, in so far as the Church has not decided upon them, claim only human credence.

✠ ✠ ✠

Articles Used for Holy Mass and Their Spiritual Significance

THE Catholic Church, jealous of the inestimable treasure which her Divine Bridegroom entrusted to her in Holy Mass, the Sacrifice of the New Law, has laid down minute rules, called *rubrics,* as to the *place* where the Sacrifice should be offered, the altar and its furnishings, the sacred vessels, linens and other articles to be used, and the vestments to be worn by the priest in its celebration. Every Catholic ought to have at least a general knowledge of what these articles are, their use in the Mass, and their spiritual significance, not only in order to be able more fully to enter into the spirit of the adorable Sacrifice, but also to be able to instruct non-Catholic inquirers, many of whom, if they were better acquainted with the beauties of our religion, would readily embrace its doctrines.

We alone can say with Saint Paul: *"Habemus altare—*We have an altar," and a true Sacrifice. Of all the blessings bequeathed by Jesus Christ to His Church, there is none better, none greater, none holier than the holy Sacrifice of the Mass. And since Holy Mass is the highest act of public worship, it is proper that it should be celebrated with fitting sacred ceremonies.

First of all, there is the *church* or chapel itself, the house of God where the people assemble to worship and where the adorable Sacrifice is offered. According to the law of the Church, Holy Mass should be celebrated only in a church or in a chapel which has been lawfully blessed, but with special permission it may be offered also in other places, for instance, in private houses, on board ships, in halls, etc. A Catholic Church is a most sacred place, dedicated to God's service by special ceremonies and blessings,

Articles Used for Holy Mass and Their Spiritual Significance

1. Ciborium
2. Chalice
3. Censer or Thurible
4. Incense Boat
5. Baptismal Shell
6. Paten
7. Kiss of Peace
8. Canopy for Ciborium
9. Ewer
10. Inclined Candelabra
11. Bishop's Candlestick
12. Ostensorium
13. Box for Hosts
14. Ablution Cup
15. Holy Oil Bottles
16. Poor Box
17. Holy Water Font
18. Chain for Beadle
19. Ciborium for Viaticum
20. Bell
21. Collection basket
22. Altar Cross
23. Holy Water Pot
24. Holy Water Sprinkler
25. Ampulla for Holy Oil
26. Cruets and Plate
27. Clapper for Signals

28. Holy Oil Bottle and Plate
29. Missal Stand
30. Bishop's Sandal
31. Bishop's Glove
32. Bishop's Ring
33. Altar Card
34. Processional Cross
35. Stole
36. Thabor
37. Banner
38. Candlestick
39. Mitre
40. Sanctuary Lamp
41. Alb
42. Dalmatic
43. Chasuble
44. Cope
45. Bishop's Rochet
46. Lectern
47. Maniple
48. Swiss Guard Cane
49. Verger's Rod
50. Processional Lantern
51. Case for Relics
52. Bishop's Pectoral Cross
53. Celebrant's Chair
54. Station of the Cross
55. Choir Stall
56. Canopy
57. Baptismal Font
58. Altar
59. Votive Candelabra
60. Pulpit
61. Halberd
62. Crozier

wherein Our Lord Himself dwells day and night in the Sacrament of His Love and daily renews in an unbloody manner His Sacrifice of Calvary. Some churches are consecrated with holy oils and solemn ceremonies, and thus dedicated to God in an even more solemn and intimate manner.

The Altar and Its Furnishings

*C*HIEF among the furnishings of the church is the *altar,* which is absolutely necessary for the lawful celebration of Holy Mass. The styles of altars are as varied as the forms of church architecture, but all must have an *altar-stone* in which the relics of saints are encased. Some altars are built in a solid, permanent manner so that they cannot be moved, and are called *fixed* altars; others are so arranged that the altar-stone can be removed and are called *portable altars.* In the former, the table must be a single slab of stone firmly joined by cement to the support, so that the table and support together make one piece. The latter are in common use among missionaries. The altar-stone may be only a slab of stone about ten by twelve inches in dimension, fitted into a wooden table at the center where the Sacred Host and Chalice are placed, or the entire table may be a slab of marble. Five crosses are engraved upon the surface—one at each corner and one in the center—symbolic of the five Holy Wounds of Christ. Since the altar is the place whereon the holiest of sacrifices is offered to God, it must be dedicated to God's service in a special way. It is therefore consecrated by the bishop with long prayers and solemn ceremonies, with the use of holy oils, incense and holy water.

The altar stands on an elevation called the *predella*, with steps leading up to it, reminding us of Mount Calvary upon which the Bloody Sacrifice of the Cross was consummated. The *Crucifix* upon the altar likewise reminds us that the Sacrifice offered here is the same as that once offered upon the Cross.

On the altar table rests the *tabernacle*, the receptacle in which the vessels containing the Blessed Sacrament are reserved. The name of *tabernacle*, or tent, given to the Eucharistic habitation of Our Lord, is taken from the sacred tent of the Israelites which served as their sanctuary before the erection of Solomon's Temple. Dear to every Catholic heart is this sacred enclosure, which harbors within its walls the Divine "Prisoner of Love."

The rubrics require that the altar table, usually called the *"mensa"* be covered with three white linen cloths in reverence for the Most Holy Eucharist; the two lower ones are usually about the same size as the altar table; the top one extends to the floor on both sides of the altar and to a becoming distance in the front. The latter, usually adorned with dainty lace or embroidery, provides opportunities for loving fingers to ply their skill in order to beautify the sanctuary of the Lord. These cloths are symbolic of the linens in which the sacred Body of Christ was wrapped when laid in the tomb. They are blessed by the bishop or one duly authorized, and are provided to absorb the Precious Blood should the chalice be accidently overturned.

Among the principal ornaments of the altar are the candles, which are lighted during the celebration of Holy Mass and other services. At a Low Mass said by a priest, the Church prescribes that two candles are to be used; at a Low Mass said by a bishop, four; at a High Mass sung by a priest, six; at a Solemn Pontifical Mass celebrated in the bishop's own diocese, seven; and at a Mass offered before the Most Blessed Sacrament exposed, not fewer than twelve. On occasions of greater solemnity, such as first class feasts of the Church, additional candles may be used. The candles required for Holy Mass must contain a notable portion of pure, bleached beeswax, and must be blessed. In lighting the candles for Mass, the rubrics prescribe that the acolyte should first light those on the Epistle side, commencing at the tabernacle, and then those on the Gospel side.

The burning candle is a beautiful symbol of our Lord Jesus Christ, the Light of the World. The pure wax formed by virgin bees from the pollen of fragrant flowers is symbolic of Christ's pure Body, born of the Immaculate Virgin Mary; the wick represents His Soul, and the flame, His Divinity. Furthermore, the lighted candle typifies very beautifully the hearts of the faithful, fragrant with virtue, pure, loving the Divine Sun and being illuminated by It. Likewise, we may behold in the burning candle a symbol of the three theological virtues: The light represents *Faith*, which dispels the darkness of unbelief; its rising heavenward typifies *Hope*, which continually tends upward to the possession of the joys of heaven; the glowing flame symbolizes *Charity*, which should burn in our hearts for God and for our neighbor and consume us by its ardor. These are the virtues which ought especially to animate our souls during Holy Mass.

Lighted candles add to the solemnity and beauty of the Divine services, and are a symbol of the joy of the Church on festive occasions. Needless to say, they are supported by candlesticks and candelabra whose beauty and costliness depend upon the means or generosity of the people and the solemnity of the occasion on which they are used.

The Sacred Vessels

NEXT in importance to the altar itself are the sacred vessels which are used for the celebration of Holy Mass and other services. These consist of the following:

1. The Chalice

The *chalice* is the cup-like vessel which contains the wine and water, and after the Consecration, the Precious Blood of Jesus Christ. How precious ought not this vessel to be to serve so exalted a purpose! The Church prescribes that it should be of gold or silver, if possible. But if poverty does not permit, an inferior metal may be used, though in such case the inside of the cup must be heavily gold-plated. The chalice reminds us of the cup which Our Lord used at the Last Supper when He instituted the Blessed Sacrament. It receives its name from the Latin word *calix,* meaning a *cup.*

2. The Paten

The *paten* is a small plate of the same material as the chalice, upon which the altar bread is offered at the Offertory, and later, the Sacred Host. Both the chalice and paten must be consecrated by a bishop, who anoints them with holy chrism. Before they are purified by the priest, after use at Mass, only one vested with Holy Orders may touch them.

These sacred vessels, holding the Body and Blood of Christ, may remind us of the sepulchre in which that sacred Body was enclosed for three days; and the precious metal of which they are fashioned should remind us that our hearts should be adorned with the gold of charity in order to be worthy receptacles for the Sacred Body and Blood of Christ in Holy Communion. The word *paten* is derived from the Latin, *patena*, a flat dish.

3. The Ciborium

The *ciborium* is a chalice-like vessel with a cover, which contains the small Sacred Hosts for the people's Communion. This should be of gold, if possible, or at least gold-plated inside, and must likewise be blessed. It receives its name from the Latin word *cibus,* meaning *food.* When the particles have been consecrated and it rests with its precious contents within the tabernacle, it is covered with a silk drapery, either white or gold in color, which is removed when the priest distributes Holy Communion.

4. Cruets and Other Small Vessels

The *cruets* are the two small flasks in which the water and wine used in the celebration of Holy Mass are contained. These are usually of glass so that the two fluids may be easily distinguished, but they may also be of precious metal if desired. A small *basin* and *towel* are provided for the washing of the priest's fingers. These articles are handed to the celebrant by the acolyte at the required time, and are usually kept on a small table near the altar, called the *credence table.* The *ablution vase* is a small vessel containing water for purifying the priest's fingers after he has touched the Sacred Host. A small finger towel always lies near this vessel.

5. The Missal and Missal-stand

The *Missal* or Mass-Book is the large book which contains the prayers and Gospels recited during Holy Mass. When the altar is prepared for the celebration of Mass, the Missal is placed on the Missal-stand at the Epistle side of the altar, with the opening toward the tabernacle. The prayers contained in the Missal are very beautiful. Many of them have been compiled from the Bible, and have been gathered by the Church through the ages. They are usually printed in black letters, while the rules which guide the priest at the celebration of the Mass are printed in red. These rules are called *rubrics,* from the Latin word *ruber,* which means *red.*

6. The Altar-cards

Three *altar-cards,* one placed on the Epistle side, another on the Gospel side of the altar, and one in the center, have certain parts of the Mass printed upon them to serve as an aid to the priest's memory.

7. The Monstrance

The *monstrance* or *ostensorium* is a beautiful, richly wrought vessel, executed in various forms and designs, in which the Sacred Host is exposed for Benediction of the Blessed Sacrament and for public adoration. In the center of this vessel there is a receptacle, called the *lunula* or *lunette* — a little gold case, circular or crescent in shape, in which the Sacred Host reposes when placed in the monstrance. This is removable and usually has glass covers. It may remind us of the chaste bosom of the Virgin Mary whereon the Incarnate Son of God reposed and was exhibited to the first adorers, the shepherds and the Magi. Like the chalice and the paten, it may remind us, too, of the beauty that should adorn our hearts when our Eucharistic

Lord comes to take up His abode within our souls, and that by our conduct we ought to show forth Christ dwelling within us, just as He is shown forth in the monstrance.

8. The Censer

The *censer* or *thurible* is a vase-shaped vessel of precious metal with cover suspended by chains, used for burning incense at solemn offices of the Church. Glowing coals are placed in this vessel, and when the incense is sprinkled upon these coals, opaline clouds waft heavenward and fill the whole edifice with their delicate fragrance. Incense is a granulated aromatic resin obtained from certain trees in eastern and tropical countries. Burning incense has always been regarded as a symbol of prayer. Our hearts may be compared to thuribles in which glows the ardor of Divine love, and from which the incense of prayer and praise rises heavenward to descend again in the form of grace and blessings. The sweet fragrance of the incense is symbolic of the fragrance of virtue which ought to enhance our prayer and of the complacency with which God regards the prayer of pure, loving hearts.

Incense is burned at Solemn High Mass to give greater solemnity to the Service, and is also used at Benediction of the Blessed Sacrament. The censer takes its name from the Latin word, *incendere, to burn;* and *thuribulum, incense holder.*

9. The Incense Boat

The *incense boat* is a small, boat-shaped, covered vessel, which contains the incense, and a small spoon with which to put the incense into the censer.

10. The Pyx

The *pyx* is a small metal case used for carrying the Blessed Sacrament to the sick. It is usually placed in a pouch which is suspended from the neck of the priest and rests on his bosom. This vessel may also be looked upon as a sacred vessel of the altar, since it is used as a container for the Sacred Host.

11. The Communion Paten

The *Communion paten* may also be mentioned, the use of which in connection with a communion cloth has been prescribed by recent legislation. It is a small plate, with or without a handle, which is held by the communicant under the chin while receiving and then carefully passed to the next person. It may also be carried by a server.

12. The Sanctuary Lamp

The Church prescribes that one, three or a greater uneven number of lights be kept constantly burning before every altar where the Blessed Sacrament is reserved. Usually a lamp is suspended in the middle of the sanctuary, with a red glass, so the the flame emits a crimson glow, reminding us of the love of the Sacred Heart abiding in the tabernacle. The sanctuary lamp should be fed with olive oil or beeswax, but where these are not easily procurable, the use of other oils may be permitted by the Ordinary.

Linens and Coverings for the Sacred Vessels

IT IS strictly prescribed that only pure linen should be used about the altar in accordance with a venerable custom which owes its origin to the fact that the Body of Our Lord was wrapped in linen before being laid in the sepulchre. Linen is emblematic of sincerity and purity of heart. The linens used in connection with the sacred vessels are:

1. The Corporal

The *corporal* is a square white linen cloth, about fifteen by fifteen inches, upon which the Sacred Host and chalice rest during Holy Mass, and upon which the monstrance is placed at Benediction of the Most Blessed Sacrament. It derives its name from the Latin word *corpus,* meaning *body,* because the Body of Our Lord rests upon it. The corporal receives a special blessing. When not in use, it is folded and placed in the burse.

2. The Pall

The *pall,* a piece of linen about six or seven inches square, usually stiffened with cardboard, is used as a protection over the chalice. The pall, like the corporal, is blessed.

3. The Purificator

The *purificator,* a small, oblong piece of white linen, is draped over the chalice at the beginning and again at the end of Holy Mass. It is used for cleansing the interior of the chalice and the paten and to dry the priest's fingers. The purificator is washed by a person in Sacred Orders before being entrusted to lay persons for laundering. This linen need not be blessed.

4. The Burse

The *burse* is a small square case or pouch, formed by joining two square pieces of material stiffened with cardboard, with an opening at one side. It is used as a container for the corporal, and is placed upon the chalice as the last of its coverings. It is made of the same material and corresponds in color to the vestment which the priest wears, and bears the figure of a cross or other sacred image. When the priest distributes Holy Communion outside of the time of Holy Mass he brings with him a burse containing a corporal, where-on to place the ciborium while it rests on the altar.

5. The Chalice Veil

The *chalice veil* is a large, square cloth, of the same material and color as the vestments of the priest, used as a covering for the chalice. It may have a figure of a cross on the portion which is draped in front of the chalice. At the beginning and at the completion of Holy Mass, the chalice veil is draped over the chalice; during Holy Mass, while not in use, it is folded and laid aside.

The Sacred Vestments

BY THE command of God, the priests of the Old Law wore special vestments in the discharge of their sacred functions. With how much greater reason should not the priests of the New Law make use of special vestments, particularly while offering the holy Sacrifice of the Mass, when it is remembered that the sacrifices of the Old Law were merely types and figures of the one Sacrifice of the New Law, and received all their virtue and efficacy from the Victim of Calvary, who is therein immolated anew upon the altars.

Ecclesiastical writers tell us that nothing positive is known concerning the vestments worn by the Apostles and their priestly successors in the performance of the Eucharistic Service during the first days of the Christian dispensation. The Council of Trent, however, declares that the use of vestments in the Holy Church rests on "Apostolic prescription and tradition." The Mass vestments are adaptations of the secular attire commonly worn in the early Christian centuries. In the East, men formerly wore long, loose garments reaching to the ankles, and gathered about the waist with a cincture or girdle. The Apostles and the priests in the early days wore this style of garment for everyday use, but while performing the Divine service, as might be expected, they would lay aside their ordinary apparel and put on garments of the same style but of better material. Gradually these garments were enriched with costly ornamentations, and in the course of time their style changed until the vestments became as we see them today.

Before use, the Mass vestments are blessed either by the bishop or the priest, who thus dedicates them to God's direct service. They signify the office and duty of the priest as well as the sentiments which should animate his heart while performing the sacred functions. The sacred vestments worn at the altar are the following:

1. The Amice

The *Amice* is an oblong piece of fine linen which the priest puts on first to cover the head, then the neck, and then spreads it over the shoulders under the alb. Formerly it was worn as a hood until the priest arrived at the altar, when it was lowered and thrown back over his shoulders. This custom is still retained by the Benedictines, Dominicans, Franciscans and Carmelites.

The word "amice" is derived from the Latin *amicire*, to put on a garment, or to cover. It was introduced as an ecclesiastical vestment in the eighth century, to cover the neck, which until that period had been left bare.

The amice should be made of pure, fine linen, measuring thirty-six by twenty-five inches. It should have a small cross stitched in the center upon its upper edge, and strings sewn or fastened at each end, sufficiently long to cross over the breast and encircle the body. This vestment (because it was originally used to cover the head), signifies the recollection that should characterize the priest in speech and sight. Hence, even today, at the ordination of a sub-deacon, this vestment is first placed, not on the neck, but on the head of the ordained, and the bishop pronounces the words, "Receive this garment, whereby restraint of the tongue is signified."

When the priest puts on this vestment before Holy Mass he first lets it touch his head, and prays: "Place, O Lord, upon my head the helmet of salvation, that I may overcome the attacks of Satan."

2. The Alb

The name *alb* is derived from the Latin word *albus*—white. The alb was adopted into the liturgical service in the first ages of Christianity when it was a robe worn in ordinary life. Its form has always been a wide linen garment covering the whole body and reaching to the feet. As linen receives its brilliant whiteness only through hard labor, the spotless alb indicates that purity of heart is obtained and preserved only by earnest labor and mortification.

The alb represents the humanity of Jesus Christ, in whose place the priest approaches the altar. It signifies also the white robe with which Herod clothed our Savior. This vestment is likewise a symbol of the stainless internal justice which ought to adorn the priest who immolates the spotless Lamb upon the altar. Therefore the priest, while putting on the alb, prays: "Make my soul white, O Lord, and my heart clean, that, purified in the Blood of the Lamb, I may enjoy eternal delights."

3. The Girdle or Cincture

The *girdle* or *cincture*, a cord made of linen or wool, is worn around the waist to gather the alb, thereby to facilitate movement. According to Dr. Rock it signifies the ropes

THE TREASURES OF THE MASS

Angelic Servers. *St. John Chrysostom asserts: "During the celebration of the sacred Mysteries, the altar is surrounded by angels who unite to honor Jesus Christ, the sacrificed Lamb of God." The same saint affirmed he had no difficulty in believing that the angels, arrayed in dazzling garments, encircle the altar, "for where the King is, there is His court."*

"Can a believing Christian doubt," asks St. Gregory, "that at the moment of consecration, at the words of the priest, the heavens open, and the multitudes of angels descend to honor, by their presence, the sacred Mysteries in which Jesus Christ sacrifices Himself for us?" St. Augustine declares, "Angels even condescend to surround the priest as servants, in order to assist him in his sublime function."

with which Jesus was bound when taken captive. It is in more modern times only that the girdle has been generally made like a cord. In ancient times it was flat and broad. It was not always white but varied in color and not infrequently was woven of gold, richly embroidered and studded with precious stones, as may be gathered from various authorities.

The girdle or cincture is a symbol of priestly continence and chastity. In wearing it, the priest obeys the words of Christ: "Let your loins be girt" (Luke 12: 35). The two ends united typify the two means, watchfulness and prayer, which must be combined to acquire chastity and self-restraint. "It is then that we gird our loins," says the holy Pope Gregory the Great, "when by continence, reticence and temperance we hold our sensual body in restraint."

When girding himself with the cincture, the priest prays: "Gird me, O Lord, with the cincture of purity, and extinguish in my loins the fires of concupiscence, that the virtue of continence and chastity abide within me."

4. The Maniple

The word *maniple* is said to be derived from the two Latin words *manus* and *pleo*, properly meaning "a handful" or "a bundle."

The maniple, worn on the left arm, symbolizes the cords with which Our Lords hands were bound, and signifies the penitential, laborious and indefatigably active life led by the priest. Originally the maniple was a strip of linen suspended from the left arm like a napkin carried by attendants at table. It was used to wipe perspiration from the face and brow occasioned by heat, fatigue, or labors of the ministry, and for all the purposes of a modern pocket-handkerchief. Hence, it was sometimes called *sudarium*.

After the maniple had, in the course of time, become too ornamental for the fulfilment of its original purpose, it was retained as a symbol of the sacred calling of the ministry. Towards the eighth century it began to be made of the same material as the stole and chasuble.

By the ninth century, deacons as well as priests wore the maniple. Since the twelfth century subdeacons have received it as the insignia of their office, and they are required to wear it as an honorable badge of their ministerial office at the solemn service of High Mass.

When putting on the maniple the priest prays: "Let me merit, O Lord, to bear the maniple of tears and sorrows, so that I may receive with joy the reward of all my labors."

5. The Stole

The stole consists of a strip of material, usually silk fabric, about eighty inches long and from two to four inches wide. It signifies the cross placed upon the shoulders of our Savior, and is symbolic of the priestly dignity and power. It also signifies the spiritual vesture of justice and immortality, of which we were stripped by original sin and which our Savior regained for us through His atonement.

During the first eight centuries the stole was called *orarium,* derived from *orare,* "to pray," as was the robe which the primitive Christians invariably wore during the time of public prayer, and with which the female portion of the congregation could veil their heads, according to the admonition of St. Paul (1 Cor. 11: 5). When the stole became peculiar to the ministers of the altar it ceased to be made of linen, but was fashioned of the same material as the chasuble. As in the Latin, so in the Greek and Oriental Churches, the stole is a very conspicuous ornament amongst the vestments peculiar to the higher ministers of the altar.

The stole is adorned with three crosses: one in the center which the priest kisses before putting it on, and one at each end. The vestment is placed round the neck, falling over the breast, there the two halves cross each other and are fastened securely with the cincture. The crossing of the stole on the breast signifies the yearning of the priestly soul for the love of God, which was lost by Adam's fall and regained by the death of Christ on the Cross. When the priest wears the surplice, the stole is allowed to hang straight down on both sides. Thus worn, it reminds the priest of his daily duty of expending his energy enthusiastically for the cause of Christ. Now, enthusiasm springs from love, and service born of love reveals itself in self-sacrifice for the sake of the Master.

The one thought, then, in the priest's mind when putting on the stole should be *service*. And that he may serve God with clean hands and a pure heart he prays for the innocence and immortality which man had when he came from the hands of his Creator; *"Return to me, O Lord, that robe of immortality which I have lost by the prevarication of our first parents, and although unworthy to approach Thy holy Mystery, nevertheless may I merit joy eternal."*

6. The Chasuble

The principal vestment of the priest is the *chasuble*, which serves as an outer garment and covers nearly all the other vestments. It is symbolic of the purple garment which was placed on Our Lord's shoulders in the courtroom of Pilate. This vestment was developed from a garment worn in primitive ages, called the *paenula*. The latter was a garment of a simple circular shape, with an opening in the center to allow the head to pass through. It was made large enough to fall about in rich folds, completely enveloping the person of the wearer. Its use in Rome succeeded that of the toga, and from its amplitude and encompassing form it was doubtless one of the most chaste and unassuming in appearance of the secular robes of the period. Hence we may understand why the early Christians adopted it as best fitted to be worn during the sacred offices, regarding it, at one and the same time, as symbolical in its roundness and fulness of the never-ending joys of the faithful followers of the Savior and the plenitude of love of the Eternal Father.

This vestment later came to be known as the *chasuble,* derived from the Latin word *casula,* which means "a little hut." It was so called because it entirely enveloped the figure of the wearer. When the ample chasuble was worn, the deacon held up its side during the elevation and other solemn parts of the services, to relieve the arms of the celebrant; and thus an act which was at one time of necessity is now, owing to the curtailed dimensions of the vestments, practiced as a mere symbol of old usage.

The chasuble retained its full amplitude for many centuries, because a sufficient number of attendants assisted the celebrant; but when the celebration of the Liturgy, or Mass, became more frequent, and the priest daily offered up the Holy Sacrifice unattended by a deacon and other ministers, he experienced the inconvenience of the chasuble, which formed, when extended, a perfect circle unbroken by any opening, and fell round the body in such a manner as to envelop it completely. Gradually it took on the proportions of the chasuble with which we are familiar today.

Although the chasuble was at one time a common robe of the clerics, still for many centuries it has been regarded in a special sense as the sacerdotal vestment and as a vestment intended exclusively for the Holy Sacrifice, since the priest at his ordination is solemnly invested with it. When placing the folded chasuble on the back of the newly ordained priest, the bishop says: "Receive the sacerdotal garment, by which love is understood; for God is powerful to increase in thee charity and a perfect work." Afterwards, when fully unfolding the chasuble, he says; *"With the garment of innocence may the Lord clothe thee."* The chasuble signifies the yoke and burden of Christ, as also the holy and ample charity with which the priest, like his Divine Master, should embrace all men, and yet conceal it as under a mantle.

The chasuble is adorned with a large cross in the front and the back, recalling to mind the Cross which Our Lord carried to Calvary and on which He offered Himself for our salvation. The spiritual significance of this cross is beautifully expressed in the *Imitation of Christ*: "The priest, clad in his sacred vestments, is Christ's vice-regent, to pray to God for himself and for all the people in a suppliant and humble manner. He has before him and behind him the sign of the Cross of the Lord, that he may always remember the Passion of Christ. He bears the cross before him in his vestment, that he may diligently behold the footsteps of Christ, and fervently endeavor to follow them. He is marked with a cross in back that he may suffer mildly, for Christ's sake, whatsoever adversities may befall him from others. He wears the cross before him that he may bewail his own sins; and behind him, that through compassion he may lament the sins of others; and know that he is placed as it were a mediator between God and the sinner."

When attiring himself with the chasuble, the priest says: *"O Lord, Thou who hast said: 'My yoke is sweet, My burden light,' grant that I may carry this yoke and burden in such a manner as to obtain Thy grace."*

Clad in these vestments,—three (amice, alb and cincture) of linen, and three (maniple, stole and chasuble) of some other material, which varies in color according to the day or feast, — the priest approaches the altar. He carries in his hands (under the veil with its burse) the chalice, paten, host, pall and purificator. In the burse resting on the veil lies the corporal, which is spread out over the altar stone upon the priest's arrival at the altar. With the altar itself prepared, candles lighted, the credence table set with water, wine and linen, all is in readiness for the celebration of Holy Mass.

7. The Cope

The *cope* is a long, flowing vestment, shaped like a cloak, open in the front, and having a sort of cape of the same material attached to it, which is usually adorned with ornamental designs and fringes. Necessity, not splendor, introduced this robe amongst the sacred vestments. In the early days of the Church, the Popes were accustomed to assemble the people at some particular church on certain occasions. Thence the Pope proceeded with the people, on foot, to one of the more celebrated basilicas of Rome, to hold what was called a "station." On such occasions the Pontiff wore what was called a *pluviale*, or cope, to protect him from rain and bad weather. This garment came to be employed at the altar, and has ever since been worn by bishops and priests on different occasions, particularly at the celebration of Vespers and Benediction of the Most Blessed Sacrament. The cope is usually of silk or velvet, and fastens on the breast with clasps. It corresponds in color with the vestments of the day.

8. The Dalmatic and Tunic

At solemn High Mass, solemn processions and Benedictions, the deacon and subdeacon wear vestments called the *dalmatic* and *tunic* respectively, except when these services have a penitential character. The dalmatic has been regarded from earliest times as a festal garment. It is a robe with wide sleeves, reaches to the knees and is closed in front and back, being open on the sides as far as the shoulders. The under side of the sleeves are slit, so that the dalmatic becomes a mantle like a scapular, with an opening for the head, and two square pieces of material falling from the shoulder over the arm. It is generally made of silk, corresponding to the chasuble of the priest, with which it agrees also in color.

The dalmatic is the distinctive outer vestment of the deacon. In vesting the deacon with this garment, the bishop prays: *"May the Lord clothe thee with the garment of salvation and with the vesture of praise, and may He cover thee with the dalmatic of righteousness forever."*

The vestment assigned to the subdeacon in his ministry at the altar is called the *tunic*. Were the regulations of the Church followed in all their precision, this garment would be longer, but not so ample as the dalmatic of the deacon. However, according to a custom which everywhere prevails, both these vestments perfectly resemble each other.

Bishops, when they pontificate at High Mass, wear the tunic and the dalmatic (made of lighter material) under the chasuble, to signify the fullness of the priesthood.

9. The Cassock and Biretta

The *cassock* and *biretta* are not vestments, strictly so called, but they form part of the vesture of priests and clerics. The cassock or soutane, as it is sometimes called, is a long gown or robe reaching to the ankles, and buttoned all the way down the front. In Catholic countries it is worn also on the street. The cassock of priests and clerics is black; that of cardinals, bishops and prelates worn at home is black with red or purple trimmings. Cardinals wear a red cassock in church; bishops and prelates, purple. The cassock worn by the Pope is white. Boys and laymen assisting at religious services may also wear a cassock.

The *biretta* is a stiff, square cap, with three or four ridges on its upper surface. It is worn by the clergy, whose rank is distinguished by its color, when entering or leaving the sanctuary for Holy Mass and at other functions.

10. The Surplice

Lastly, mention may be made of the *surplice,* a large-sleeved, loose tunic of half length, made of linen or cotton material, and adorned with lace or embroidery at the hem and sleeves. This is also a liturgical vestment, worn by the clergy in choir, at processions, and at Benediction. The surplice is likewise worn by those in minor orders, as also by altar boys when serving at Holy Mass and other sacred functions.

The Liturgical Colors

THE colors sanctioned by the Church for the vestments worn by her sacred ministers and the draperies used in the decoration of the altar are called *liturgical* colors. In the Roman rite, since the time of Pope St. Pius V, these colors are five in number, namely: *white, red, green, violet* and *black. Rose* color is employed only on the third Sunday in Advent (called Gaudete Sunday) and the fourth Sunday of Lent (called Laetare Sunday), to signify subdued rejoicing.

1. *White* is used on the Feast of the Blessed Trinity and on all feasts of Our Lord except those of His Passion, to signify joy and glory; on feasts of the Blessed Virgin, of the holy angels, of confessors, virgins, and all saints who are not martyrs, to signify innocence and purity. It is used also on the Nativity of St. John the Baptist, on the chief feast of St. John the Evangelist; on the feasts of the Chains and of the Chair of St. Peter, the Conversion of St. Paul, and All Saints; at the consecration of churches and altars, the anniversaries of the election and coronation of the Pope

and of the election and consecration of bishops; also for the octaves of these feasts, and from Holy Saturday till the vigil of Pentecost. White is used also for votive Masses when the feasts themselves have white, as also in services connected with the Blessed Sacrament, and for nuptial Masses and Masses at the burial of children.

2. *Red* is used on the Feast of Pentecost and during its octave; on the feasts of Our Lord's Passion, His Precious Blood, the Finding and Exaltation of the Holy Cross, and the feasts of the Apostles and martyrs; also at votive Masses of these feasts.

3. *Green,* the symbol of *hope,* is used on all days which have no special festive character and which do not denote sorrow. It is employed from the octave of the Epiphany to Septuagesima Sunday, and from Trinity Sunday to Advent, except on feasts, ember days and vigils occurring during that time.

4. *Violet* or purple is the color assigned for Advent and for the penitential season from Septuagesima Sunday till Wednesday of Holy Week (except on feasts); also for vigils and Ember days, except the Vigil and Ember days of Pentecost and the Vigil of the Epiphany; for the Rogation days; and for the Feast of the Holy Innocents, unless this feast falls on a Sunday, when red is used. Violet is used also in certain votive Masses throughout the year. It is a sign of humility, contrition and penance.

5. *Black,* the color of mourning, is used in the solemn ceremonies on Good Friday, to comemmorate the Death of Our Lord, and in the Masses of Requiem for the repose of the souls of the faithful departed.

It is not lawful to use vestments of any other color, such as blue or yellow, but vestments made of *gold* cloth may be used instead of white, red, or green vestments. The obligation of using the prescribed colors for the celebration of Mass is of precept; but in case of necessity, such as lack of vestments of the color prescribed for the day, vestments of another liturgical color may be used. It is better to say Mass in any color of vestment rather than omit doing so, and authors commonly hold that the observance of the colors of the vestments is not binding under a grave obligation.

Even when the Most Blessed Sacrament is exposed, the color of the vestments must always correspond to the feast or the season. It is unnecessary to add however, that black is never worn in the presence of the Blessed Sacrament exposed, nor are services of mourning performed in Its presence.

Thus we see that each vestment and color used by Holy Mother Church in her sacred ceremonies has a special significance. All are designed to attract our attention, to elevate our minds to God and to inspire us with a desire to remain faithful children of the Holy Catholic Church.

Assisting at Holy Mass

HOLY Church has not prescribed any set prayers or devotions for the faithful. Each one is free, therefore, to adopt such methods as best fit his devotion. However, among the many ways of assisting at Holy Mass, the one most highly recommended is that of uniting with the priest as closely as possible and praying the same prayers as he prays. The use of the Missal by the faithful is therefore highly to be recommended, if they wish to assist at Holy Mass in the most perfect and fruitful manner. The faithful should keep in mind that as co-offerers with the priest, their disposition at Holy Mass should foster a more intimate participation in the Sacrifice.

The word "liturgy," not being properly understood by many Catholics, is often falsely regarded as something too deep and mysterious for ordinary people. Nothing could be farther from the truth. Liturgy means simply the exercise of public worship according to Church regulation. It comprises all the prayers, ceremonies and functions prescribed by the Church for use in all services performed by an official minister in her name. To participate in the liturgy means to follow the Church in her worship and to take an intelligent and loving interest in her feasts, her rites and her ceremonies. This we do when we take an active part in the prayers of Holy Mass.

Throughout the prayers of the Mass, the Church gives evidence of her desire that the faithful co-operate actively with the priest in the celebration of the Holy Sacrifice. Holy Mass is not intended as the exclusive function of the priest, but as the united sacrifice of priest and people. The Church desires that all should understand and take part in this sublime oblation. For this reason she has encouraged the translation of the Missal into all popular languages, so that the best and simplest means of understanding the Mass and taking part in its rites and prayers might be placed at the disposal of the people.

Although by saying private prayers, such as the Rosary, during the celebration of the Mass, the obligation of attendance is fulfilled, it is far better to say the prayers of the Mass; for, as Blessed Pius X is reported to have said, "You must not only pray at Mass, you must pray the Mass." This holy Pope repeatedly expressed the hope that the Missal would be more commonly used by the faithful while attending Holy Mass. The Missal should be one of the prayer books most loved and esteemed by Catholics. It is a treasury of the most beautiful prayers of the Church, suited for all times and for all occasions.

Common sense itself tells us that it is improper to say prayers during the Mass which are not in harmony with those being offered up by the priest at the altar in the name of all. Why should we be occupied in saying litanies, or prayers to our guardian angels or patron saints during this time? When the Rosary is prayed in common or the Stations are said publicly, would we not think it odd if someone were to pray other prayers during that time? At Holy Mass, therefore, there should not be a diversity of individual devotions, but a united prayer and attentive participation of all in the Holy Sacrifice.

For those who are unable to use a missal or a prayer book so as to follow the prayers with the priest at the altar, it is certainly commendable to pray the Rosary devoutly, with reflection on its mysteries, or to meditate on the Passion, or to say other suitable prayers which are related in spirit to those of the Holy Sacrifice. It is the mind of the Church that each one assist in the manner best suited to his abilities. But all should devoutly unite themselves with the priest at the beginning of the Mass and at the principal parts—the Offertory, Consecration and Communion.

Since it is within the power of many of us to assist at Holy Mass every day, we ought to strive to draw as many and great graces as possible from each Mass. We shall succeed in this it from time to time we reflect on the sublimity of this Sacrifice and the beauty and significance of its prayers. In order to be successful in temporal business and to make it as profitable as possible, the first requisite is a good knowledge of the business. For the sake of gain, lively interest and effort are exerted in worldly concerns.

When there is question of participating in the Holy Sacrifice, eternal values are brought into consideration; here there is question, not of temporal gain, but of the greater honor of God and the good of immortal souls. Shall we then show less interest in assisting at Holy Mass than people of the world show in their temporal pursuits? If we exert ourselves to assist at Holy Mass frequently and fervently, we shall one day receive a glorious reward in eternity.

Benefits Derived from Assisting at Mass

THE holy fathers and doctors of the Church cannot say enough regarding the benefits which Holy Mass brings to the faithful. Saint Lawrence Justinian writes: *"Assuredly, no human tongue is capable of telling how abundant are the fruits to be derived from the holy Sacrifice of the Mass, how great the gifts and graces that flow from it. . . Through the Sacrifice of the Mass the sinner is reconciled with God, the just is confirmed in his justice, transgressions are forgiven, vices are exterminated, virtues multiplied, merits accumulated, temptations overcome."*

The holy Sacrifice of the Mass outweighs in value all other works. On this subject, Bishop Fornerus writes: *"He who, not being in a state of mortal sin, hears Mass devoutly, gains more than he who performs some arduous work for the love of God, or goes on a distant pilgrimage. And no wonder, for the most virtuous of good works derive their worth and importance from their object, that is, from that which is done by means of them. Now, what is nobler, more precious, more Divine, than the Sacrifice of the Mass!"*

The most important testimony of the benefits which the faithful derive from Holy Mass is that given by Holy Church herself in the Council of Trent (Session 22): *"We must needs confess that no other work can be performed by the faithful so holy and Divine as this tremendous Mystery, wherein that life-giving Victim, by which we were reconciled to the father, is daily immolated on the altar by priests."* Let us consider in detail some of the graces derived from devoutly assisting at Holy Mass.

1. Great Consolation Is Afforded at the Hour of Death

That the Masses we have heard during life will be a source of consolation at the hour of death was revealed by Our Lord to Saint Mechtilde: *"I declare to thee that I will be to him. who has assisted at Mass diligently and devoutly, comfort and protection at the hour of death; and whatever the number of Masses he has heard with devotion on earth, such shall be the number of blessed spirits I will send to attend upon his departing soul."*

A certain man, as the Ven. Martin von Cochem relates, had exercised great devotion to Holy Mass during his entire life and had as far as possible assisted thereat every day. When death came, he placed all his trust in the Holy Sacrifice, and with this confidence departed in peace. Shortly afterward he appeared to his parish priest, resplendent with glory, and said to him: "I am the soul of your late parishioner, for whom you are praying. By the grace of God I am an heir of eternal felicity. Although I do not need your prayers, I thank you for your charity in praying for me."

"What good works did you perform in your lifetime," the priest inquired, "by which you specially merited God's grace and favor?" "The principal good work that I did," rejoined the soul, "was my daily and devout attendance at Holy Mass."

Thus everyone who has been in the habit of assisting frequently and reverently at Holy Mass may, at the hour of death, take comfort in the thought that by offering to God so many

Masses he has rendered Him excellent and acceptable service and an oblation of great price; that he has frequently in all humility implored pardon and offered the abundant merits of the Savior in atonement for his sins. Nay, more, he may be comforted by the thought that the Son of God Himself has pleaded in union with him and for him in every Mass, giving His Precious Blood for his redemption.

He whose hope rests on these grounds trusts not in himself nor in his own merits, but in Our Lord, in whose merits and intercession he is permitted to participate in Holy Mass. He trusts, therefore, in the Passion and Death of Christ, renewed in every Holy Mass; in the Precious Blood of the Lamb mystically sprinkled upon his soul, and in the merits of Jesus Christ imparted to him in Holy Mass. He trusts in the great oblation offered by the hands of the priest and graciously accepted by the Divine Goodness. He trusts in the prayers offered by the priest, by Our Lord Himself, to God the Father for his salvation. On such stable foundations as these may we all rest our hope!

2. Pardon Is Implored at Our Judgment

"In peace in the selfsame I will sleep, and I will rest; for Thou, O Lord, hast singularly settled me in hope" (Ps. 4: 9,10). These words of the Psalmist may be fittingly placed on the lips of the dying Christian who during his lifetime has loved Holy Mass dearly, heard it devoutly, offered it with a pure intention and assisted at it with regularity. With confidence he may hope to meet a merciful Judge, since he has so many times offered up to Him the acceptable Sacrifice of justice, rendering Him infinite satisfaction, infinite honor, infinite delight and infinite reparation for the oftenses and sins he has committed.

It is related that a pious brother, who had died and was restored to life, confided to St. Boniface, Archbishop of Mayence, that when he was brought before the tribunal of God, all the sins of which he had been guilty rose up before him in hideous shapes and accused him one after another. One said, "I am vainglory wherewith thou didst exalt thyself before thy brethren," Another said: "I am the spirit of lying which often made thee fall." A third: "I represent the idle words which thou didst often utter." And so on. Similarly, the good deeds which he had performed rose up in his defense.

Although we do not know what the procedure of our judgment will be upon our departure from this life, we may be certain that the sins we have committed will rise up before us in appalling array, whereas the good works we have performed will also appear to console and encourage us. And if we have been diligent and devout in assisting at Holy Mass, may we not, relying on the promise of Our Lord to St. Mechtilde, hope to behold a band of fair spirits advancing toward us, to dispel our fears and reassure us, saying: *"Recognize in us the Masses thou didst hear on earth. We will go with thee into the dread presence of thy Judge. We will speak in thy defense. We will show how deep was thy devotion, how many sins thou didst expiate and the penalties thou didst cancel. Be of good courage, we will appease the wrath of thy Judge and implore mercy on thy behalf."*

3. Venial Sins and Their Temporal Punishment Are Remitted

By devoutly assisting at Holy Mass we can obtain the forgiveness of our venial sins for which we are sorry, as well as of our unknown sins which we have never confessed. Likewise we can diminish the temporal punishment due to our sins, according to the degree of our fervor. That Holy Mass is a powerful means of atonement, is asserted by St. Thomas Aquinas in these words: *"The special effect of the holy Sacrifice of the Mass is that it operates our reconciliation with God."* In explanation of this statement he gives the following illustration: *"Just as a man will forgive the wrong done him by his fellow-man in consideration of a valuable gift which is presented to him, or a service which is rendered, so the anger of God may be appeased by the acceptable service thou dost render Him when thou hearest Mass, and by the priceless gift which thou dost offer Him in the oblation of the Body and Blood of Jesus Christ."*

Such is the frailty of our corrupt nature that we daily fall into many sins, seeming scarcely to take heed of them. Although they may be for the most part venial offenses, they are nevertheless deplorable in the sight of the all-holy God, and we shall one day have to render an account and make satisfaction for each of them. How consoling, then, are the words of the spiritual writer, Marchantius: *"It is evident that in accordance with the object of its institution, the holy Sacrifice of the Mass blots out venial sins. For Christ, knowing well how weak our nature is and how prone to evil by reason of original sin, provided us with a suitable remedy and ordained a daily sacrifice for dally sins."*

If we did not have this Divine oblation, or if we were to make no use of it for the expiation of our sins, alas! what a weight of guilt should we not carry with us before the tribunal of the Eternal Judge! How long, how severe, would be the atonement required from us in the next world!

St. Gertrude was accustomed at the elevation of the Sacred Host, to offer the adorable Victim for the washing away of her sins, saying simply: *"Holy Lord God, I offer to Thee this Sacred Host for the remission of my sins."* So acceptable was this oblation in the sight of God the Father that He graciously admitted the saint into His embrace. Let us, too, often assist at Holy Mass and offer to God the Father the sacred oblation of His Divine Son for the atonement and obliteration of our sins, saying: Most merciful Father, since this sacred Victim is the most true and worthy atonement for the guilt of mankind, vouchsafe to receive It in expiation of my sins, and grant me remission of the chastisement due to them.

The following words addressed by Our Lord to St. Gertrude show how easily we may obtain remission of our sins through offering Holy Mass for this end: *"If thou believest that I was offered up to God the Father upon the Cross because it was My will to be offered in this manner, believe also and doubt not that every day I desire, with the same love and strength of desire, to be sacrificed for every sinner upon the alter as I sacrificed Myself upon the Cross for the salvation of the world. Therefore, there is not one, however heavy the weight of sin wherewith he is burdened, who may not hope for pardon if he offers to the Father My sinless life and death, provided he believes that thereby he will obtain the blessed fruit of forgiveness."*

The spiritual writer, Marchantius, says again: *"The holy Sacrifice of the Mass, offered to Almighty God, serves to atone for mortal sins, but pre-eminently for secret sins — those which after careful examination of conscience we cannot recall to mind."* Holy Mass does not actually cleanse from grievous sins, but it obtains for us the grace of contrition, not only for known sins, but still more for those which are unknown or forgotten. That we have cause for apprehension on account of these sins is shown by the words of St. Paul: *"For I have nothing on my conscience, yet I am not thereby justified; but He who judges me is the Lord"* (1 Cor. 4: 4).

Thomas Aquinas teaches also that the holy Sacrifice of the Mass has the power to remit temporal punishment due for our sins, because by this Sacrifice "the fruits of the bloody Sacrifice of the Cross are distributed and received in the most abundant measure" (Council of Trent). The measure of the atonement, however, is proportionate to our worthiness and the manner in which we attend the Holy Sacrifice.

4. The Conversion of Sinners Is Effected

That the holy Sacrifice of the Mass is likewise efficacious for the conversion of sinners is proved by the following revelation to St. Gertrude. One day, when the saint was earnestly entreating God at the time of Mass to prevent with His grace those souls who were destined to be converted and saved, and in virtue of the Holy Sacrifice to anticipate the time fixed for their conversion, she longed to plead also for those reprobate sinners who appeared to be doomed to eternal perdition, so great was the compassion she felt for them. She restrained herself, however, fearing that she would pray in vain. Our Lord, desiring to correct this want of confidence on her part, said to her: *"Do you suppose that My spotless Body and Precious Blood here upon this altar is not sufficiently powerful to bring those who are in the way of perdition to a better course of life?"*

St. Gertrude, amazed at the excess of loving-kindness evinced by these words, felt emboldened, while pondering them in her heart, to cry to the all-merciful Savior, imploring Him by His sacred Body and Blood, by the Holy Mass then being celebrated, by His perpetual oblation of Himself upon the altar for the salvation of sinners, to bring at least some of those sinners who were in the way of damnation back to a state of grace. Our Lord graciously received her fervent petition, and assured her that it would be granted.

According to the teaching of theologians. God gives in Holy Mass preventing grace, by virtue of which the sinner is brought to the knowledge and abhorrence of mortal sin. This Divine assistance, merited by the Mass heard or celebrated, does not, however, produce the same effect in all. There are hardened sinners and sinners who are inclined to penance. The latter will, by Holy Mass, be brought to true contrition and penance, and thus be reconciled to God; but the former, though the same grace is offered them, may reject it in the obduracy of their evil hearts.

The holy Sacrifice of the Mass does not always effect the conversion of the sinner at once; usually it works gradually, when God softens the hard heart of the sinner by degrees, and disposes it to receive the influence of grace. Oftentimes it happens that by a special grace the sinner is converted after the lapse of some time and is not aware that he owes his conversion to the potency of the Holy Sacrifice.

Holy Church also teaches that when a repentant sinner offers the holy Sacrifice of the Mass to God, with the intention of conciliating Him, the grace of conversion and reconciliation with God will certainly be granted him. By so doing, many sinners have obtained the grace of repentance, which otherwise they would not have obtained. Were She not well aware that the offering of this expiatory Sacrifice has the power to soften the hardened heart and to convert the obstinate sinner, Holy Church would not place upon the lips of her priests the following prayer; *"Be appeased, we beseech Thee, O Lord, by our offerings which Thou hast accepted; and graciously compel our wills, even though rebellious, to turn to Thee"* (Secret, 4th Saturday of Lent).

5. Virtue and Sanctifying Grace Are Increased

Through the holy Sacrifice of the Mass, the infused virtues of faith, hope and charity are increased in us, and the inspiration and assistance of Divine grace applied to our souls, so that we are the better able to resist temptation, perform penance more willingly, practice virtues, increase our merits, and are more certain of persevering to the end in grace. Truly, may it be said that every Holy Mass is a pulsation of the Sacred Heart of Jesus, which conveys His Lifeblood to all the members of His Church. Every grace which converts a sin-stained soul into a beloved child of God has its source on the altar. The cleansing Blood which invisibly washes away the most grievous sins in the confessional, preserves from eternal punishment and restores to the soul the white robe of sanctifying grace, springs from the Savior's fountains on the altar. For there is present, really and truly, the Fountain of the Precious Blood which flows unto the end of the world.

The Fathers of the Church state expressly that God rewards with very special graces those who devoutly assist at Holy Mass. St. Cyril says: *"Spiritual gifts are freely given to those who assist at Mass reverently."* And Pope Innocent III writes: *"Through the power of the holy Sacrifice of the Mass, all virtues are increased in us, and we obtain a plenteous share of the fruits of grace."*

"Christians should never neglect Holy Mass," says St. Maximus, *"because of the grace of the Holy Ghost, of which all who are present are made partakers."* And Fornerus declares: *"The potency of the merits of Christ's Passion is most forcibly felt in Holy Mass, in procuring for us graces and celestial riches in marvelous abundance."*

In giving us His Divine Son in Holy Mass, God the Father gives us at the same time all His merits and the satisfaction He made for sin. He gives us His Flesh and Blood, His Body and Soul, and all the treasures which He has earned. Now, whenever we offer to the Heavenly Father these precious gifts in Holy Mass, we count out to Him, as it were, coins wherewith to purchase heavenly riches, and a great increase of Divine grace. And if we remember the words of St. Thomas Aquinas, that one single grace is a greater good than all the good things of the whole world, we will realize how easily we can amass heavenly treasures if we assist frequently and devoutly at the adorable Sacrifice of the Mass.

6. Our Heavenly Glory Is Augmented

Our Lord once revealed to a privileged soul that every time a person hears Holy Mass devoutly, he increases and lays up merit for eternal life. And as it is the infallible teaching of Holy Church that all the good works of one who is justified, merit an increase of grace and of glory, it may be confidently affirmed that by every Holy Mass heard with a certain amount of devotion one may gain for oneself a higher degree of glory in heaven. Just as when we climb an eminence we reach a greater elevation at every step, so each time we hear Mass we merit a higher place in heaven, and the height which we attain is greater or less in proportion to the fervor of our devotion. The higher our place in heaven, the nearer we shall be to God, and the clearer will be our knowledge of Him, the more ardent our love for Him and the more abundant our enjoyment of Him. Each degree we rise will increase our beauty, our brilliance, our nobility, our riches, our glory, and the esteem in which the saints will hold. us.

If we were to hear Holy Mass every day of our lives with fervent devotion, to what a height of glory might we not attain? What riches, what felicity, would be ours to enjoy for all eternity! And if sometimes we had occasion to hear two or three Holy Masses in one day, what an increase of glory would be ours!

7. God's Blessing Is Secured in Temporal Affairs

Unless the Divine blessing rests upon our labors, they will meet with no true success. Now, there is no better means of obtaining an abundant blessing from God than by assisting at Holy Mass. Our Lord bestows His benediction upon all who go to Mass; He blesses their work and all they do. A pious writer says: *"He who begins the day by going to Mass will be attended by better success in his work, in his business, in whatever his hands find to do, or wherever his feet carry him."*

The time we take from our daily occupations to spend in the service of God is not wasted, as so many seem to believe. On the contrary, it is very well employed and earns for us from God a temporal and an eternal reward. Has He not told us with His own Divine lips: *"But seek first the kingdom of God and His justice, and all these things shall be given you besides"*? (Matt. 6: 33.) This is equivalent to saying: Hear Mass in the morning and you shall have an abundant blessing on all you do during the day.

When we hear Mass devoutly and offer it to God, we render Him an infinite service, infinite honor, infinite satisfaction. We present to Him a gift so costly that all treasures of heaven and earth cannot compare with it. By no means will God allow this great service, this precious gift, to go unrewarded. Many instances are related in which Catholics were visibly blessed in their temporal affairs by devout attendance at Holy Mass.

The ecclesiastical historian Baronius tells us that in the early ages of Christianity, priests were at liberty to say as many Holy Masses every day as they wished. The holy Pope Leo III had recourse to the Holy Sacrifice in all his necessities, and was known, in times of affliction, to celebrate no less than nine Masses in one day, with great fervor and recollection.

8. Relief and Release for the Poor Souls

Holy Mass, the greatest act of homage man renders to God, is likewise the most efficacious means of relief and release for the holy souls in purgatory. It is not only the unbloody Sacrifice of atonement for the living, but also the expiatory Sacrifice for the suffering souls in purgatory. The holy Fathers teach that many souls go forth from purgatory every time Holy Mass is celebrated, and St. John Chrysostom says: *"As often as Holy Mass is celebrated, the angels of heaven hasten to open the gates of purgatory."*

In the august Sacrifice of the Mass, it is the Body and Blood of Jesus Christ, an infinite treasure of satisfaction, which is offered to the Heavenly Father for the living and the dead. The Blood of Christ cries for mercy and pardon, and Its cleansing streams flowing into the realms of purgation bring unspeakable relief to those imprisoned there. The suffering souls themselves have repeatedly given testimony of this. Thus we read that in the time of St. Bernard a deceased religious appeared to his brethren and thanked them for having released him from a long purgatory. When asked what had brought him the greatest relief in his torments, he pointed to the altars, saying: *"Behold, there are the weapons of Divine grace, by which I was released. There is shown the power of Divine mercy; there is the price of my ransom which enables me now to enter into heaven."*

When we assist at Holy Mass, our Savior gives us the very key to the superabundant treasury of His merits and His mercy; He permits us to open this treasury and to take away as much as our devout dispositions enable us to receive. Could we but see how the poor souls are refreshed and released through the power and efficacy of the Holy Sacrifice, how we would hasten in Christian charity to have this atoning Sacrifice offered up for them and to assist at it in their behalf.

SOME HELPFUL REMINDERS

Neglected Practice of Devotion

Not only ought we to be assiduous in assisting at Holy Mass, but also in having Holy Masses offered for our various needs, both spiritual and temporal. Only too true are the words of a pious writer who speaks thus of our neglect in this regard: *"The devotion of having the Divine Mysteries celebrated, which ought to have its place of honor above all other devotions, often holds a very inferior place. To obtain contrition for sin, the remission of temporal pains, or to obtain a certain favor, recourse is had to prayer, or to some chosen act of piety, but rarely to the celebration of the Holy Sacrifice. The Blessed Virgin will be invoked, the angels and saints, above all, those in vogue, but rarely one thinks of having the Holy Sacrifice offered, which is the most powerful means of propitiation, of satisfaction, of impetration. And what one does not do for oneself, one forgets for others. There are among those dear to us, guilty souls, souls in debt, souls in danger. We deplore and weep, yet neglect the means above all which can expiate all, redeem all, pay all, obtain all. . ."*

"A man gains much more by having Mass said for himself in his lifetime than by simply hearing Mass," says Father Martin von Cochem. Those who contribute some service to the celebration of the Mass such as the choir, the organist and the servers, and especially the celebrant himself, participate in richer measure in the fruits of the Holy Sacrifice. In like manner, the person who has Holy Mass said for his intention shares more abundantly in the graces and blessings of the Mass than one who merely assists thereat. This measure of grace is increased still more if the person who has the Holy Mass offered also assists at it.

Advantages of Having Masses Said During Our Lifetime

Many devout Catholics are solicitous to have Holy Masses celebrated for the repose of their souls after their death. For this purpose they save money and make provision in their last will to have a portion of their estate devoted to the offering of Holy Masses. This is good and praiseworthy, and persons acting thus should by no means be dissuaded from doing so. Yet it is far more profitable and meritorious to have Holy Masses celebrated for oneself during life. According to St. Anselm, a single Mass offered up in one's lifetime is equivalent to many after one's death. St. Leonard of Port Maurice likewise declares that one Mass before our death is much more profitable to us than many after it. The following are the reasons given in support of this assertion:

1. If we have a Holy Mass said for ourselves during our lifetime, we are the cause of its celebration and can assist at it, thus adding to our merit. This would be impossible after our death.
2. If a Holy Mass is celebrated for us during our lifetime, and we are perhaps in the state of sin, we may hope to receive from God's mercy, in virtue of this Mass,

the grace to realize our sinful state, to be moved to true contrition and to reconcile ourselves to God by a sincere confession. This would be impossible after death, for if we were to die in mortal sin, even thousands of Masses would not procure our return to the state of grace. We should forever remain enemies of God and children of wrath—How terrible it is to think that there are doubtless many souls in hell who would not be there if Masses had been said for them during their lifetime!

3. Holy Mass can obtain for us the grace of a happy death, for if we have Masses said for this intention, God will lend us special aid to triumph over the enemy of our souls in that decisive hour. We must, however, join our own co-operation to the pious practice of having Masses celebrated. For, to have Masses said to obtain the grace of a good death, and at the same time to live a worldly life or not make efforts to leave the path of sin, would be to run the great risk of not obtaining the grace we ask. To the Masses said must be added the frequentation of the sacraments, and above all, it possible, assistance at these Masses and participation in them fully by receiving Holy Communion.

4. The merit of the Holy Masses which are said for us during life will accrue to our benefit and will gain for us a higher degree of glory in heaven. But even if thousands of Masses were celebrated for us after our death, our heavenly glory would not be increased by one degree; for in heaven merits are no longer placed to our credit.

5. One Holy Mass said for us during our lifetime will do more to free our souls from the punishment of sin than many said for us after death. For our sojourn in

this world is a time of grace, but afterwards comes the time of just retribution. A slight penance voluntarily performed in this world has more value in the sight of God than compulsory penance of much greater severity in the world to come. The Holy Masses which are said for us during our lifetime will go before us into eternity to cancel, either in whole or in part, the punishment due for our sins. We shall thus either be preserved entirely from purgatory or our punishment will be mitigated or shortened. For by every Holy Mass we pay to God a great part of our indebtedness, so that we may reasonably hope to escape a great part of our punishment after death.

In the next world the time of grace ceases. God judges everything according to the rigor of His justice. Accordingly, every venial sin is punished so severely that many Masses may not suffice to cancel what one alone would have cancelled during our lifetime. Moreover, if we defer having Holy Masses said until after our death, we shall be obliged to wait for their celebration, and this waiting will be most distressing and painful in case we are in purgatory. From apparitions of poor souls to pious persons we learn that one hour in purgatory seems to them as years in this world. Hence it is better that the benefits accruing to us from Holy Mass be obtained in advance than that we be obliged to wait for them in the torments of purgatory.

This does not mean, however, that we can have Holy Masses said during life to be applied to our souls after death, for Holy Mass cannot be applied in view of a future contingency. Theology does not permit us to suppose that God holds in reserve, in His treasury, until the day of particular judgment, the satisfactory fruit of the Mass to apply it to the soul upon leaving the world. We ought therefore to put into practice the wise counsel of Cardinal Gennari, which is, not to have all the Holy Masses celebrated at one time, but to have them celebrated at frequent intervals during our lifetime; for the satisfactory value of Holy Mass applies only to sins already committed at the time of its celebration—not to those committed afterwards.

6. By having Holy Mass said during our lifetime we make an offering in the form of a stipend for the support of the priest, thereby depriving ourselves of some means of gratification or even of necessity and acquiring the additional merit of sacrifice. After death we deprive ourselves of nothing, for then our earthly enjoyments have ended and our means go to our heirs. In making bequests for Masses after our death, our action no longer includes self-denial; we give what we shall inevitably be deprived of by death. Hence our offering cannot be so pleasing to God and so meritorious for ourselves as it would have been if we had made it during our lifetime.

Appropriating the Threefold Efficacy of the Mass

It may be well to mention here a fact which is often overlooked, or perhaps not generally known. When a person has Holy Mass offered in honor of some saint; or to obtain some petition, he asks for the Mass for the special intention which he has in mind, but does not think to appropriate to himself or to another person the satisfaction or merit of that Mass.

Let us remember that Holy Mass has a threefold efficacy: 1. Satisfactory, 2. Propitiatory, and 3. Impetratory. If we have a Holy Mass offered for the poor souls, only the satisfactory merit redounds to their benefit—that is, the remission of punishment due to sin. The propitiatory merit, which appeases the just anger of God against sinners and cleanses the soul from venial sin and imperfection, may at the same time be applied for the conversion of a sinner or to the benefit of our own soul. And the impetratory merit, which implores God for graces and favors, may be directed toward the obtaining of some grace or blessing, such as a cure from sickness, employment, a happy hour of death, etc.

Similarly, if we have a Holy Mass offered to honor some mystery of our holy religion or in honor of a saint, we may at the same time include separate intentions for the application of the satisfactory, propitiatory and impetratory fruits of the Mass. It we neglect to do this, we are told, we shall not draw as rich benefits from the Holy Sacrifice as we should have done had we made such intentions. If the priest also omits to do this, and the satisfaction of the Holy Mass is not applied to anyone in particular, it will probably go to the treasury of the Church, unless God, in His goodness, applies it to those who, through ignorance, have neglected to appropriate it to themselves.

Assisting at Several Masses at the Same Time

It is regrettable that many pious persons hold the opinion that nothing more is to be gained by hearing two or more Masses at one and the same time than if one Mass alone were heard. This is an erroneous opinion which robs them of many spiritual treasures.

According to the teaching of eminent theologians, two or more Masses may be heard at the same time with as much profit and advantage as if they were heard separately.[14] Thus,

---

[14] *This, however, would not fulfil one's obligation if one had promised to hear two or more Holy Masses for a certain intention, or if they had been enjoined as a penance. In such case, the Masses would have to be heard consecutively and not simultaneously.*

one who enters a church at a time when several Masses are being celebrated may unite his intention with all the Masses and participate in the fruits of each.

We know that during each Holy Mass the celebrant prays for all those present; the angels who are always in adoration in large numbers wherever a Holy Mass is being offered, likewise add their intercession for those persons who are present. But above all, it is the supreme High Priest, Christ Himself, who makes Himself the advocate of each individual who assists at Mass. He lays the needs of each one in particular before God, and for each one He offers His sacred Body and Blood. Therefore, if we have the intention of assisting at two or more Masses, even though they be said at the same time, in each of these Masses He pleads for us; He grants us a share in His merits; He nourishes us spiritually with His Body and Blood; He bestows upon us a greater degree of grace here and of glory hereafter; He gives us His heavenly benediction. And the more Masses we hear, the more are these favors multiplied.

It must be understood, however, that it does not suffice to be merely bodily present in the Church while several Masses are being offered; we must unite our intention with each one, adore Christ on each altar, and offer Him to God the Father with the desire to assist at each Mass. During the time of the Consecration at each altar, we should adore our God present there, and our own interests demand that we should offer this precious Gift to God the Father, for all our needs and intentions. If two or more priests should reach the Consecration at the same moment, we may make the intention of adoring Christ present on all the altars at the same moment. Should we not be able to see the priests or the Sacred Hosts, we are always able to hear the bell which is rung at the Consecration, and thus in spirit unite with the priest and make our acts of adoration and oblation. Thus we will gain immense treasures which will be ours to enjoy for all eternity.

Uniting in Spirit with All the Holy Masses Being Offered throughout the World

Those who are prevented from being actually present at the celebration of Mass may yet draw glorious fruits from this great ocean of grace. For we may assist in spirit at the adorable Sacrifice, just as we may receive Holy Communion spiritually with great profit to our souls. In fact, we may be physically a long distance from the churches where Mass is being offered, and yet be spiritually nearer than one who assists in a careless, distracted manner. And just as we may now offer to God, with great benefit to our souls, the sufferings which our Blessed Savior endured so many centuries ago, so we may likewise offer up the many Holy Masses which are being continually celebrated day and night, and thereby become partakers in the innumerable graces of the Holy Sacrifice.

It is a glorious, but alas! a sadly unheeded truth, that no moment of the day or night passes but that the Lamb without stain is offered on many altars. In all these oblations of infinite value, we may participate—by having the heartfelt desire to do so. Our good desires are before God as if we really carried them out, and the more fervently we unite in spirit with all the Holy Masses being offered throughout the world, the greater will be the benefits we reap. Statistics show that on an average there are four Elevations every second of the day and night—each one of infinite value, and each one of which we may offer to the Most Holy Trinity for our own needs, the wants of Holy Church, the conversion of sinners, and for the suffering souls in purgatory. Thus, also, we may offer to God an unceasing homage of praise, adoration, thanksgiving, and petition, in our own name and in the name of all creatures. What a sublime privilege it is that even while our hands are busily engaged in our daily occupations, our hearts and our wills may unite with the angels and the faithful who surround the altars whereon the adorable Sacrifice is being offered. Ah! let us then frequently renew our intention of uniting our prayers, our works, our sufferings with the sacred Oblation of Christ offered on all the altars throughout the world, and let us draw from this richest treasury the infinite fruits of His unbloody Sacrifice. Thus the perpetual immolation of the Lamb of Sacrifice, the very many Masses offered every twenty-four hours, will become in truth our very life, an inexhaustible source of graces for ourselves and the world of souls, and an offering of infinite value for the glory of the Triune God. For there is nothing greater than Holy Mass to give to God for His glory, or to win heaven's highest gifts for ourselves and for souls.

Acts of Oblation

Morning Offering

O MY God, I wish to offer Thee this day, without ceasing, all the Masses that are now said, have been said, or ever will be said, until the end of time. In union with them, I offer Thee all my thoughts words, and actions, joys and sorrows, each breath I draw, each beat of my heart, to Thine everlasting praise and glory, to Thine infinite rejoicing and delight, for the glory and honor, praise and love of the Sacred Heart of Jesus; to thank Thee for all the graces bestowed on Our Blessed Lady; to make Thee infinite reparation for my own sins and the sins of the whole world; to render Thee infinite thanksgiving for all Thy benefits to myself and to all creation, and to obtain for each and all, every best grace and blessing. Through each drop of the Precious Blood in all these Masses thus united, I beg for the conversion of sinners, help for the agonizing, relief for the souls in purgatory, and zeal and holiness for priests. Amen.

Offering before Holy Mass

Eternal Father, I offer Thee the Sacrifice wherein Thy dear Son Jesus offered Himself upon the Cross and which He now renews upon this altar, to adore Thee and to render to Thee that honor which Is Thy due, acknowledging Thy supreme dominion over all things and their absolute dependence on Thee, for Thou art our first beginning and our last end; to give Thee thanks for countless benefits received; to appease Thy justice provoked to anger by so many sins, and to offer Thee worthy satisfaction for the same; and finally to implore Thy grace and mercy for myself, for all those who are in tribulation and distress, for all poor sinners, for the whole world and for the blessed souls in purgatory. [15]

---

[15] *Indulgence of 3 years for devoutly making this act of oblation at the beginning of Mass. ("Manual of Indulgences," 68.)*

www.ingramcontent.com/pod-product-compliance
Lightning Source LLC
Chambersburg PA
CBHW072344100426
42738CB00049B/1634